Brandee Jankoski

Easy Eats

Delightful Dishes for Every Meal, Plus Creative Leftover Ideas

Copyright © 2023 by Brandee Jankoski

All rights reserved. No part of this publication may be reproduced, stored or transmitted in any form or by any means, electronic, mechanical, photocopying, recording, scanning, or otherwise without written permission from the publisher. It is illegal to copy this book, post it to a website, or distribute it by any other means without permission.
First edition

This book was professionally typeset on Reedsy.
Find out more at reedsy.com

Contents

1 Introduction

Welcome Note	11
Purpose of the Cookbook	11
Who This Cookbook is For	11

2 Kitchen Essentials

Essential Equipment and Tools	14
Stocking Your Pantry	14
Common Ingredients and Substitutes	15
Seasonal Produce Guide	15
Basic Techniques Explained	16
Glossary of Cooking Terms	17

3 Sauces and Dips

Simple Guacamole Recipe	21
Avocado Salsa Recipe	22
Traditional Salsa Recipe	23
Spicy Buffalo Dip	24
Classic Marinara Sauce	25
Szechuan Sauce Recipe	26
Sauce for Shrimp and Fish Tacos Recipe	27
Chile Verde Sauce Recipe	28
Sweet and Spicy Asian Marinade	29

Japanese Mayo Salad Dressing	30
Homemade Ranch Dressing Recipe	31
Tzatziki Sauce Recipe	32
Mango Chutney Recipe	33
Spicy BBQ Sauce Recipe	34
Classic Basil Pesto Recipe	35
Homemade Tartar Sauce	36
Classic Remoulade Sauce	37

4   *Appetizers and Sides*

Buffalo Chicken Wings Recipe with Oven and Air Fryer Options	41
Potato Skins Recipe	42
Egg Rolls Recipe	43
Classic Nachos	44
Artichoke Spinach Dip Recipe	45
Classic 7-Layer Dip Recipe	46
Classic Crab Cake Appetizer	47
Classic Burger Slider	48
Buffalo Chicken Slider	49
BBQ Chicken Slider	50
Homemade Macaroni and Cheese	51
Homemade Garlic Naan Recipe	52

5   *Soups and Salads*

Homestyle Chicken Noodle Soup	57
Hearty Beef Minestrone Soup	58
Hearty Italian Wedding Soup	59
Traditional Clam Chowder	60
Hearty Split Pea Soup	61

Garden Salad Recipe	62
Spinach Strawberry Salad with Feta and Candied Pecans	63
Classic Caesar Salad	64
Wedge Salad Recipe	65
Classic Coleslaw	66
Fresh Corn, Black Bean, and Feta Salad with Avocado	67
Cobb Salad Recipe	69
Chinese Chicken Salad Recipe	71
Macaroni Salad Recipe	72
Greek Pasta Salad Recipe	73

6 Breakfast and Brunch

Eggs in the Basket	79
Breakfast Sandwich Recipe with Sriracha Mayo	80
Fried Eggs, Bacon, and Potato Breakfast with Toast	81
Scrambled Eggs, Bacon, Potato, and Cheese Breakfast Burrito	84
Bacon, Cheese, and Avocado Omelette	86
Denver Omelette	88
Spanish Omelette with Chorizo and Cheese	90
Steak and Eggs Skillet (see Dinners)	93
Chilaquiles with Corn Tortilla Chips, Beans, Cheese, and Fried Eggs	94
Breakfast Tostada Recipe	97
Spinach and Parmesan Quiche Recipe	98
Traditional Pancakes	99
Banana Nut Oat Pancakes	100
Blueberry Pancake Recipe	102
Classic French Toast Breakfast	103

7   *Dinner and Leftover Recipes*

Herb Roasted Chicken and Vegetables	111
- Chicken and Veggie Quesadillas Using Leftovers	112
Chicken Parmesan with Fettuccine Pasta and Caesar Salad	113
- Chicken Parmesan Sandwich with Fettuccine Soup Using Leftovers	116
Chicken Piccata Recipe with Asparagus and Rice Pilaf	117
- Chicken Piccata Sandwich Using Leftovers	119
Spatchcock Chicken with Potatoes and Brussels Sprouts Recipe	120
- Chicken Enchiladas Using Leftovers	122
Stuffed Chicken Breast with Mozzarella, Pesto, and Sun-Dried Tomatoes	123
- Leftover Stuffed Chicken Panini Using Leftovers	125
Sticky Asian Chicken Legs with Asian Cabbage Salad and Fried Rice	126
- Asian Chicken Lettuce Wraps Using Leftovers	128
Orange Chicken Recipe with Fried Rice	129
- Orange Chicken Lettuce Wraps Using Leftovers	132
Chicken Tikka Masala with Jasmine Rice, Chutney, Garlic Naan, and Creamed Spinach	133
- Chicken Tikka Masala Wrap Using Leftovers	135
Chicken Curry with Broccoli Casserole Recipe	136
- Chicken Curry Broccoli Casserole Sandwiches Using Leftovers	137
Baked Chicken Breast Dinner with Corn and Carrots Recipe	138
- Chicken Pot Pie Recipe Using Leftovers	140

BBQ Chicken Thighs with Ranch Potato Bake
and Wedge Salad 141
- BBQ Chicken and Ranch Potato Casserole Using Leftovers 143

Stuffed Pork Tenderloin Dinner 144
- Pork Tenderloin Sandwich Using Leftovers 147

Stuffed Pork Chops with Garlic Mashed Potatoes
and Honey Glazed Carrots 149
- Creamy Pork Pasta Using Leftovers 151

Slow Cooker BBQ Baby Back Ribs with Pasta Salad
and Potato Salad 153

Leftover BBQ Rib Sandwiches 155

Slow Cooker Pulled Pork Recipe with Corn on the Cobb 157
- Pulled Pork Tacos Using Leftovers 159

Slow Cooker Pork Chile Verde Recipe 160
- Pork Chile Verde Burrito with Black Beans,
Rice, and Fried Eggs Using Leftovers 162

Breaded Pork Chops, Homemade Macaroni and
Cheese, and Green Beans 163
- Pork Chop Mac and Cheese Casserole Using Leftovers 165

Herb-Crusted Steak with Garlic Mashed Potatoes
and Honey-Glazed Carrots 166
- Steak and Eggs Skillet Breakfast Using Leftovers 167

Beef with Broccoli Recipe 168
- Beef and Broccoli Stir-Fry Wraps Using Leftovers 170

Steak and Shrimp Fajitas Recipe 172
- Fajita Breakfast Hash Recipe Using Leftovers 175

Meatloaf with Mashed Potatoes and Peas Recipe 177
- Meatloaf Sandwich Recipe Using Leftovers 178

Slow Cooker Pot Roast with Sourdough Rolls — 179

- Pot Roast Pie Using Leftovers — 181

Shepard's Pie Recipe — 183

- Shepard's Pie Stuffed Rolls Recipe Using Leftovers — 184

Classic Lasagna Recipe — 185

- Lasagna Soup with Garlic Bread Croutons Using Leftovers — 188

Jambalaya Recipe — 190

- Jambalaya Stuffed Peppers Recipe Using Leftovers — 192

Ground Beef Taco Recipe — 193

- Taco Soup Recipe Using Leftovers — 195

Homemade Spaghetti and Meatballs with Sauce — 197

- Meatball Sub Casserole Using Leftovers — 199

Basil Shrimp Pasta Recipe — 201

- Creamy Basil Shrimp Fritatta with Caesar Salad Croutons Using Leftovers — 204

Tilapia Dinner with Baked Potato and Broccoli — 205

- Fish Taco Recipe Using Leftovers — 207

Shrimp Linguini Recipe — 209

- Shrimp Linguini Stir-Fry — 211

Sautéed Salmon with Rice Pilaf and Steamed Broccoli — 212

- Salmon Salad Using Leftovers — 213

8 Desserts

Vanilla Cake Recipe — 219

Chocolate Cake Recipe — 221

Carrot Cake with Cream Cheese Frosting Recipe — 223

Caramel Cheesecake Recipe — 225

Peanut Butter Caramel Cheesecake — 227

Pecan Praline Silk Supreme Pie — 229

Chocolate Chip Cookies Recipe	233
Simple Sugar Cookies Recipe	235
Classic Peanut Butter Cookies Recipe	237
Classic Snickerdoodles Recipe	239
Strawberry Shortcake	241
Apple Cake	244
Banana Bread	246

Introduction

Welcome Note

Welcome to "Easy Eats: A Beginner's Guide to Cooking"! I'm thrilled to embark on this culinary journey with you. Whether you're stepping into the kitchen for the first time or looking to expand your cooking skills, this cookbook is designed to guide, inspire, and empower you through every chop, stir, and simmer.

Purpose of the Cookbook

Welcome to "Easy Eats," the cookbook designed for the modern home cook looking for simplicity, flavor, and efficiency in the kitchen. This collection celebrates the joy of home-cooked meals without the fuss, focusing on delicious dinners that effortlessly transform into tomorrow's lunch. We've intentionally omitted a separate lunch chapter because we believe in the art of repurposing. Each dinner recipe has a creative twist on turning your evening's effort into a brand-new midday delight. From cozy family meals to quick solo plates, "Easy Eats" invites you to reduce food waste, save time, and enjoy the double delight of cooking once and relishing twice. Get ready to embark on a culinary journey that simplifies your meal planning and amplifies your taste experience—one dinner and leftover makeover at a time.

Who This Cookbook is For

"Easy Eats" is for anyone and everyone who wants to start cooking but doesn't know where to begin. It's for the college student living on their own for the first time, the busy professional who wants to eat healthier, the parent who wants to prepare quick and nutritious meals for their family, or even the seasoned home cook looking for easy and delicious recipes to add to their repertoire. No matter your age, cooking skill level, or culinary preference, this book is a friendly companion in your culinary adventure.

Let's tie on our aprons, roll up our sleeves, and get ready to discover the joy of cooking. Your journey to becoming a confident home cook starts here!

Kitchen Essentials

Essential Equipment and Tools

Building a well-equipped kitchen doesn't require a lot of gadgets. Here are the essential tools you'll need to start cooking delicious meals:

- **Knives:** A chef's knife, a paring knife, and a bread knife should cover most of your cutting needs.
- **Cutting Board:** Opt for at least one large, sturdy cutting board, preferably wood or plastic.
- **Pots and Pans:** A set of pots and pans should include a large stockpot, a saucepan, and a couple of frying pans (one non-stick, one regular).
- **Mixing Bowls:** A set of mixing bowls of various sizes comes in handy for prepping and mixing ingredients.
- **Baking Sheets and Casserole Dishes:** Essential for baking and roasting.
- **Measuring Cups and Spoons:** Precision is key in cooking, so these are a must.
- **Can Opener and Vegetable Peeler:** Basic but indispensable tools.
- **Spatulas and Wooden Spoons:** For stirring, flipping, and mixing.
- **Colander:** For draining pasta and washing vegetables.
- **Grater:** Useful for cheese, vegetables, and zest.
- **Thermometer:** An instant-read thermometer ensures meats are cooked to the right temperature.

Stocking Your Pantry

A well-stocked pantry is the foundation of good cooking. Here are essentials to keep on hand:

- **Oils and Vinegars:** Olive oil, vegetable oil, and a basic vinegar like white or apple cider.
- **Spices and Herbs:** Salt, black pepper, garlic powder, onion powder, dried basil, oregano, cumin, and chili powder are a good start.
- **Canned Goods:** Canned tomatoes, beans, and broths are versatile staples.
- **Grains and Pasta:** Rice, pasta, and a variety of grains like quinoa or barley.
- **Flour and Baking Essentials:** All-purpose flour, baking soda, and baking powder.
- **Sugars:** White and brown sugar.
- **Dairy:** Milk, butter, and a variety of cheeses.

- **Eggs:** Useful for countless recipes.
- **Frozen Vegetables:** Handy for when you don't have fresh veggies.
- **Bread and Crackers:** For quick snacks and sides.
- **Condiments:** Ketchup, mustard, soy sauce, and any other favorites.

With these tools and pantry staples, you'll be well on your way to cooking a variety of dishes. Remember, cooking is a journey, and your kitchen will evolve with your skills and preferences. Happy cooking!

Common Ingredients and Substitutes

Sometimes you might find yourself missing an ingredient while cooking. Here's a list of common ingredients and their substitutes to help you in a pinch:

- **Butter:** Substitute with margarine or for baking, use applesauce or mashed bananas for a healthier option.
- **Eggs:** For baking, use a "flax egg" (1 tablespoon of ground flaxseed mixed with 3 tablespoons of water) or mashed bananas.
- **Milk:** Almond, soy, and oat milk are good dairy-free alternatives.
- **All-purpose Flour:** Use whole wheat flour or for a gluten-free option, try almond or oat flour.
- **Sugar:** Honey, maple syrup, or agave nectar can be used as natural sweeteners.
- **Baking Powder:** Mix ¼ teaspoon baking soda with ½ teaspoon cream of tartar.
- **Oil:** For frying, use canola or vegetable oil. For salads, olive oil or avocado oil are great.
- **Sour Cream:** Greek yogurt is a healthier alternative with a similar texture.
- **Herbs:** If a recipe calls for fresh herbs and you only have dried, use one-third the amount specified (1 tablespoon fresh = 1 teaspoon dried).

Seasonal Produce Guide

Eating seasonally ensures that you get the freshest and most flavorful produce. Here's a basic guide to what's in season throughout the year:

- **Spring:** Asparagus, strawberries, cherries, peas, radishes, rhubarb, artichokes, spinach.
- **Summer:** Tomatoes, corn, cucumbers, bell peppers, peaches, water- melon, zucchini, berries, eggplant.

- **Fall:** Apples, pumpkins, squash, sweet potatoes, Brussels sprouts, pears, cranberries, grapes.
- **Winter:** Citrus fruits, kale, leeks, turnips, potatoes, winter squash, pomegranates, dates.

Remember, this guide can vary based on your location and climate. Visit local farmers' markets to discover what's in season in your area. Seasonal produce not only tastes better, but it's often more affordable and environmentally friendly.

Understanding ingredients and their substitutes can make cooking less daunting and more creative. Plus, knowing what produce is in season will enhance the flavor of your dishes and might even inspire you to try new recipes!

Basic Techniques Explained

1. **Chopping and Dicing:** Chopping refers to cutting ingredients into irregular pieces, while dicing means cutting into uniform cubes. Use a sharp knife and a stable cutting board.
2. **Sautéing:** Cooking food quickly in a small amount of oil or butter over medium-high heat. It's great for vegetables, meat, and seafood.
3. **Boiling:** Cooking food in boiling water. This method is commonly used for pasta, eggs, and vegetables.
4. **Simmering:** Cooking liquid at a temperature just below boiling. Bubbles form but don't burst the surface. Ideal for soups and sauces.
5. **Roasting:** Cooking food in an oven at a high temperature. Vegetables and meats are often roasted to enhance flavor.
6. **Baking:** Cooking food through dry heat in an oven. This technique is mostly used for bread, pastries, and casseroles.
7. **Grilling:** Cooking food over direct heat. This can be done on a grill or using a grill pan on the stove.
8. **Blanching:** Briefly boiling food and then plunging it into ice water. It's used to soften vegetables, or to peel fruits and nuts.
9. **Marinating:** Soaking food in a flavorful liquid for a period of time to infuse flavor and tenderize.
10. **Kneading:** Working dough with your hands to develop gluten. This is essential for bread and pizza dough.

Glossary of Cooking Terms

- **Al Dente:** Italian term used to describe pasta that is cooked to be firm to the bite.
- **Braise:** Slow cooking method where food is first browned in fat, then cooked, covered, in a small amount of liquid at low heat.
- **Caramelize:** Slowly cooking sugars in foods (especially fruits and onions) until they become brown and flavorful.
- **Deglaze:** Adding liquid (such as wine or broth) to a pan to loosen and dissolve the food particles that are stuck to the bottom.
- **Fold:** Gently combining a light, airy mixture (like beaten egg whites) with a heavier one. This is done with a spatula in a gentle lifting and turning motion.
- **Julienne:** Cutting vegetables into thin, matchstick-like strips.
- **Mince:** Cutting food into very small pieces, finer than chopping.
- **Poach:** Cooking food gently in liquid just below the boiling point.
- **Reduce:** Boiling down a liquid to decrease the volume and concentrate flavors.
- **Sear:** Cooking the surface of meat quickly at a high temperature so it forms a brown crust.

Understanding these basic techniques and cooking terms is a foundation for becoming a skilled cook. They provide the building blocks for creating a wide range of dishes and enable you to follow recipes with greater ease and confidence.

Sauces and Dips

Embark on a flavorful journey in our "Sauces and Dips" chapter, the secret realm where every culinary enthusiast can find the alchemy that turns ordinary meals into extraordinary experiences. This is where we unlock the full potential of condiments, those magical concoctions that can transform the simplest ingredients into a symphony of flavor. Whether you're seeking to add a burst of zest to a dish or create a centerpiece for your snack table, this collection has it all. From the robust richness of classic marinara to the cool, creamy delight of tzatziki, and the bold kick of a spicy buffalo dip, these sauces and dips are more than mere accompaniments; they're the soul of the party. Perfect for casual family dinners, sophisticated cocktail parties, or that big game day, each recipe in this chapter is a new ticket to dip into the divine. So, grab your whisk and let's stir up some excitement—one dip at a time!

Easy Eats

Simple Guacamole Recipe

Prep Time: Not specified, but typically under 5 minutes.

Serving Size: Not specified, but typically serves 2-4.

Ingredients:

- 2 ripe Hass avocados
- Salt, to taste
- Black pepper, to taste

Instructions:

- Cut the avocados in half and remove the pits. Scoop the flesh into a bowl.
- Using a fork, mash the avocado to your desired consistency. Some prefer it chunky, while others like it smooth.
- Season the mashed avocado with salt and black pepper. Start with a small amount, then taste and adjust according to your preference.
- Mix well to ensure the seasoning is evenly distributed.
- Serve immediately or cover with plastic wrap, pressing the wrap directly onto the surface of the guacamole to prevent browning, and refrigerate until ready to serve.

This simple guacamole focuses on the creamy, rich flavor of Hass avocados, enhanced by just a touch of salt and pepper. Enjoy it with chips, on toast, or as a complement to any Mexican dish!

Easy Eats

Avocado Salsa Recipe

Prep Time: 15 minutes | Cook Time: 10 minutes | Total Time: 25 minutes

Serving Size: 4-6

Ingredients

- 4 tomatillos, husked and rinsed
- 2 jalapeños, stems removed (adjust to taste)
- 2 other types of chiles of your choice (such as serrano or poblano), stems removed
- 1 medium onion, quartered
- 2 ripe avocados, peeled and pitted
- Salt and pepper to taste

Instructions

1. Boil the Chiles and Tomatillos:

   - In a medium saucepan, add the tomatillos, jalapeños, other chiles of your choice, and the quartered onion.
   - Fill the saucepan with enough water to cover the ingredients.
   - Bring the water to a boil over high heat, then reduce to a simmer.
   - Cook for about 10 minutes or until the tomatillos and chiles are softened.

2. Blend the Ingredients:

   - Carefully transfer the boiled tomatillos, chiles, and onion to a blender or food processor.
   - Blend the mixture until it becomes a smooth sauce.

3. Add Avocado:

   - Add the peeled and pitted avocados to the blender or food processor.
   - Blend again until the avocado is fully incorporated and the salsa reaches your desired consistency.

4. Season:

   - Season the salsa with salt and pepper to taste.
   - Pulse the blender or food processor a few times to mix the seasoning evenly.

5. Jar and Freeze (Optional):

   - If you plan to store the salsa for later use, let it cool to room temperature.
   - Transfer the salsa to a clean jar with a tight-fitting lid.
   - You can store the salsa in the refrigerator for up to a week or freeze it for longer storage. Remember to leave some space at the top of the jar if freezing to allow for expansion.

Enjoy your homemade avocado salsa with boiled chiles as a versatile and flavorful addition to your meals, or as a standalone dip with chips. The freezing option makes it convenient to have delicious salsa on hand whenever you need it!

Traditional Salsa Recipe

Prep Time: 10 minutes | Total Time: 10 minutes

Servings: 4-6

Ingredients

- 4 ripe tomatoes, finely chopped
- 1 medium onion, finely chopped
- 2 cloves garlic, minced
- 2 jalapeños, seeds removed and finely chopped (adjust to taste)
- 1/2 cup fresh cilantro, chopped
- Juice of 1 lime
- Salt to taste Optional Add-ins
- 1 teaspoon ground cumin (for a smoky flavor)
- 1/2 teaspoon sugar (to balance acidity)
- 1/4 cup diced bell pepper (for added crunch) Instructions

1. Prepare Ingredients:

- Finely chop the tomatoes and onion, and place them in a medium-sized mixing bowl.
- Mince the garlic and finely chop the jalapeños, then add them to the bowl.
- Chop the fresh cilantro and add it to the mixture.

2. Mix and Season:

- Squeeze the juice of one lime over the ingredients in the bowl.
- If using, add the ground cumin, sugar, and diced bell pepper.
- Season the mixture with salt to taste.
- Mix all the ingredients until well combined.

3. Serve:

- Taste and adjust the seasoning if needed.
- Serve immediately with tortilla chips or as a topping for tacos, burritos, or grilled meats.
- If not serving immediately, cover and refrigerate. The flavors will meld and intensify over time.

Enjoy your traditional salsa as a fresh and zesty addition to any meal or as a classic appetizer!

Spicy Buffalo Dip

Prep Time: 10 minutes
Cooking Time: 20 minutes

Servings: 6-8

Ingredients:

- 2 cups shredded cooked chicken
- 1 (8-ounce) package cream cheese, softened
- 1/2 cup hot sauce (like Frank's RedHot), or to taste for spiciness
- 1/2 cup ranch or blue cheese dressing
- 1/2 cup crumbled blue cheese or shredded mozzarella cheese
- 1/4 cup green onions, chopped, plus extra for garnish
- 1 teaspoon garlic powder
- 1/2 teaspoon onion powder
- 1/2 teaspoon smoked paprika (optional for a smoky flavor)
- Salt and pepper to taste

Instructions:

1. Preheat your oven to 350°F (175°C).
2. In a large mixing bowl, combine the shredded chicken and cream cheese. Mix well until the chicken is fully coated with the cream cheese.
3. Stir in the hot sauce, ranch or blue cheese dressing, crumbled blue cheese or shredded mozzarella, chopped green onions, garlic powder, onion powder, and smoked paprika if using. Season with salt and pepper to taste.
4. Transfer the mixture to an oven-proof dish and spread it out evenly.
5. Bake in the preheated oven for 20 minutes, or until the dip is hot throughout and bubbling at the edges.
6. Remove from the oven and let it cool for a few minutes before serving.
7. Garnish with extra chopped green onions and serve with celery sticks, carrot sticks, tortilla chips, or sliced baguettes.

Enjoy your spicy buffalo dip as the centerpiece of your appetizer spread, a surefire hit for any gathering where bold flavors are appreciated!

Classic Marinara Sauce

Prep Time: 10 minutes
Cooking Time: 30 minutes

Servings: 4-6

Ingredients:

- 2 tablespoons olive oil
- 1 medium onion, finely chopped
- 4 cloves garlic, minced
- 1 (28-ounce) can of whole peeled tomatoes or crushed tomatoes
- 1 teaspoon dried oregano
- 1 teaspoon dried basil
- 1/2 teaspoon red pepper flakes (optional, for a little heat)
- Salt and freshly ground black pepper to taste
- 1 teaspoon sugar (optional, to balance acidity)
- Fresh basil leaves, torn (for finishing the sauce)
- 1/4 cup fresh parsley, chopped (optional)

Instructions:

1. Heat the olive oil in a large saucepan over medium heat. Add the chopped onion and cook until translucent and soft, about 5 minutes.
2. Add the minced garlic and cook for another minute until fragrant. Be careful not to burn the garlic.
3. Pour in the can of tomatoes. If using whole peeled tomatoes, crush them with a spoon or potato masher in the pan.
4. Stir in the dried oregano, dried basil, and red pepper flakes if using.
5. Season with salt, freshly ground black pepper, and sugar if needed.
6. Bring the sauce to a gentle simmer and cook, uncovered, for 20-25 minutes, stirring occasionally. If the sauce is splattering, partially cover the pot.
7. If you prefer a smoother sauce, you can use an immersion blender to blend the sauce directly in the pot to your desired consistency.
8. A few minutes before the sauce is finished cooking, stir in the fresh basil leaves and parsley if using.
9. Taste and adjust seasoning if necessary.
10. Serve the marinara sauce over cooked pasta, as a dipping sauce, or use it in your favorite Italian recipes.

Enjoy this classic marinara sauce, the quintessential Italian tomato sauce that's versatile and bursting with simple, fresh flavors.

Easy Eats

Szechuan Sauce Recipe

Prep Time: 10 minutes

Cooking Time: 30 minutes

Servings: Makes about 1 cup, serving size varies based on use.

Ingredients:

- 1/4 cup soy sauce
- 2 tablespoons sesame oil
- 1 tablespoon cornstarch
- 1 tablespoon water
- 2 teaspoons garlic, minced
- 2 teaspoons ginger, minced
- 2 tablespoons brown sugar
- 1 tablespoon rice vinegar
- 2 teaspoons chili flakes (adjust to heat preference)
- 1 teaspoon Szechuan peppercorns, crushed (optional for authentic flavor)
- 1 tablespoon peanut butter (optional, for a richer sauce)
- 1 tablespoon tomato paste
- 1/2 teaspoon smoked paprika (optional, for a smoky flavor)
- Salt to taste

Instructions:

1. In a small bowl, combine cornstarch and water to make a slurry. Set aside.
2. Heat sesame oil in a saucepan over medium heat. Add minced garlic and ginger, sautéing until fragrant, about 1-2 minutes.
3. Stir in the brown sugar, rice vinegar, chili flakes, and Szechuan peppercorns (if using). Cook for another minute.
4. Mix in the soy sauce, peanut butter (if using), tomato paste, and smoked paprika (if using). Bring the mixture to a simmer.
5. Whisk in the cornstarch slurry and stir continuously until the sauce thickens to your desired consistency, usually within 2-3 minutes.
6. Taste and adjust the seasoning with salt if necessary. If the sauce is too thick, add a little water to reach the preferred consistency.
7. Remove from heat and let it cool down before serving with your favorite Szechuan dishes.

This sauce can be stored in an airtight container in the refrigerator for up to a week. Enjoy it with stir-fries, as a dip, or as a marinade for meats.

Sauce for Shrimp and Fish Tacos Recipe

Prep Time: 10 minutes
Total Time: 10 minutes

Servings: 4-6

Ingredients

- 1/2 cup mayonnaise
- 1/2 cup sour cream or Greek yogurt
- Juice of 1 lime
- 2 tablespoons chopped fresh cilantro
- 1 teaspoon garlic powder
- 1 teaspoon smoked paprika
- 1/2 teaspoon cumin
- 1/2 teaspoon chili powder
- Salt and pepper to taste Optional Add-ins
- 1 tablespoon hot sauce or sriracha (for a spicy kick)
- 1 tablespoon honey or agave syrup (for a sweet touch)
- 1 tablespoon finely grated lime zest (for extra zing)

Instructions

1. Combine Base Ingredients:

- In a medium-sized mixing bowl, combine the mayonnaise and sour cream (or Greek yogurt).
- Add the juice of one lime and mix until smooth.

2. Add Seasonings:

- Add the chopped fresh cilantro, garlic powder, smoked paprika, cumin, and chili powder to the bowl.
- Mix well to ensure all the ingredients are evenly distributed.

3. Season and Customize:

- Season the sauce with salt and pepper to taste.
- If using, add the hot sauce, honey, and lime zest. Mix well to incorporate.

4. Serve:

- Add your favorite hot sauce to taste if you like.
- The sauce is ready to be used immediately on shrimp and fish tacos.
- For best flavor, let the sauce chill in the refrigerator for at least 30 minutes before serving.
- Store any leftovers in a sealed container in the refrigerator for up to 3 days.

Enjoy this versatile sauce on your shrimp and fish tacos for a delicious and flavorful addition!

Easy Eats

Chile Verde Sauce Recipe

Prep Time: 20 minutes
Cook Time: 10 minutes
Total Time: 1 hour 20 minutes

Servings:
6-8

Ingredients

- 1 1/2 pounds tomatillos, husked and rinsed
- 3 poblano peppers
- 2 jalapeño peppers (adjust to taste)
- 1 large onion, quartered
- 4 cloves garlic, peeled
- 1/2 cup fresh cilantro, roughly chopped
- 2 cups chicken or vegetable broth
- 2 tablespoons olive oil
- Juice of 1 lime
- 1 teaspoon ground cumin
- Salt and pepper to taste

Instructions

1. Roast Vegetables:
  - Preheat your oven broiler.
  - Place tomatillos, poblano peppers, jalapeño peppers, quartered onion, and garlic on a baking sheet.
  - Broil for 5-7 minutes on each side or until the skins are charred and blistered.
2. Peel and Seed Peppers:
  - Once cooled, peel the skins off the poblano and jalapeño peppers. Remove the stems and seeds. (Wear gloves to avoid irritation from the peppers.)
3. Blend Ingredients:
  - In a blender or food processor, combine the roasted tomatillos, peeled peppers, onion, garlic, and cilantro.
  - Blend until smooth. If needed, add a little broth to facilitate blending.
4. Cook Sauce:
  - In a large saucepan, heat olive oil over medium heat.
  - Pour the blended mixture into the saucepan.
  - Add the chicken or vegetable broth, lime juice, and ground cumin.
  - Season with salt and pepper to taste.
5. Simmer:
  - Bring the sauce to a boil, then reduce heat and simmer for 45-50 minutes, or until it thickens to your desired consistency. Stir occasionally.
6. Serve or Store:
  - Use the Chile Verde Sauce immediately with your favorite dishes such as enchiladas, tacos, or burritos.
  - Store any leftovers in an airtight container in the refrigerator for up to 5 days, or freeze for longer storage.

Enjoy the rich and vibrant flavors of this homemade Chile Verde Sauce, perfect for adding a zesty kick to your meals!

Sweet and Spicy Asian Marinade

Prep Time: Less than 10 minutes
(not including marinating time)

Servings:
Enough for marinating approximately
1-2 lbs of protein.

Ingredients:

- 1/2 cup soy sauce
- 1/4 cup honey
- 2 tablespoons rice vinegar
- 1 tablespoon sesame oil
- 3 cloves garlic, minced
- 1 inch piece of ginger, grated
- 1 tablespoon sriracha (or to taste)
- 1 teaspoon Chinese five-spice powder

Instructions:

1. In a bowl, whisk together soy sauce, honey, rice vinegar, sesame oil, minced garlic, grated ginger, sriracha, and Chinese five-spice powder.
2. Place chicken legs in a resealable bag or container.
3. Pour the marinade over the chicken legs, ensuring they are well coated.
4. Marinate in the refrigerator for at least 1 hour, preferably overnight for better flavor.

Easy Eats

Japanese Mayo Salad Dressing

Prep Time:

5 minutes

Servings:
Makes about 3/4 cup, serving size varies based on use.

Ingredients:

- 1/2 cup mayonnaise
- 2 tablespoons rice vinegar
- 1 tablespoon soy sauce
- 1 tablespoon sesame oil
- 1 tablespoon sugar
- 1 teaspoon grated fresh ginger
- 1 small garlic clove, minced
- 1 teaspoon sesame seeds
- Pinch of salt

Instructions:

1. In a medium bowl, whisk together the mayonnaise, rice vinegar, soy sauce, and sesame oil until well combined and smooth.
2. Add the sugar, grated ginger, minced garlic, and sesame seeds to the mixture. Whisk again until all the ingredients are thoroughly combined.
3. Taste the dressing and add a pinch of salt if needed. The dressing should have a balance of savory, sweet, and tangy flavors.
4. Store the dressing in a jar or airtight container in the refrigerator. Allow it to chill for at least 30 minutes before serving to let the flavors meld together.
5. Give the dressing a good shake or stir before using. It can be drizzled over salads, used as a dip, or as a dressing for cold noodles.
6. Enjoy your homemade Japanese mayo salad dressing with your favorite salads or as a delicious addition to your Asian-themed meals!

Note: This dressing can be customized according to personal preference. For a spicier kick, add a dash of sriracha or chili flakes.

Homemade Ranch Dressing Recipe

Easy Eats

Prep Time:

10 minutes

Servings:
Makes about 1 1/2 cups, serving size varies based on use.

Ingredients:

- 1/2 cup mayonnaise
- 1/2 cup sour cream
- 1/2 cup buttermilk or regular milk
- 1 tablespoon fresh chives, finely chopped
- 1 tablespoon fresh parsley, finely chopped
- 1 tablespoon fresh dill, finely chopped
- 1 clove garlic, minced or grated
- 1/2 teaspoon onion powder
- 1/4 teaspoon paprika (optional)
- 1/4 teaspoon white vinegar or apple cider vinegar
- Salt to taste
- Freshly ground black pepper to taste

Instructions:

1. In a mixing bowl, whisk together the mayonnaise, sour cream, and buttermilk until smooth and well-combined.
2. Add the chives, parsley, dill, minced garlic, onion powder, and paprika (if using) to the mixture. Stir to incorporate all the herbs into the dressing.
3. Pour in the vinegar and mix thoroughly. The vinegar adds a slight tang and helps to balance the flavors.
4. Season the dressing with salt and freshly ground black pepper to taste. Be sure to add a little at a time, tasting as you go to ensure the seasoning is just right.
5. For the best flavor, cover and refrigerate the dressing for at least 30 minutes before serving. This allows the flavors to meld and intensify.
6. Before serving, give the dressing a good stir. If it's too thick, you can thin it with additional buttermilk or milk until you reach your desired consistency.

This homemade ranch dressing can be kept in an airtight container in the refrigerator for up to one week. It's perfect for salads, as a dip for veggies, or as a condiment for sandwiches and burgers. Enjoy your fresh and flavorful homemade dressing!

Tzatziki Sauce Recipe

Prep Time: 10 minutes
(not including draining time for cucumber or chilling time)

Servings:
Makes about 2 cups, serving size varies based on use.

Ingredients:

- 2 cups Greek yogurt (full-fat recommended)
- 1 large cucumber, grated and drained
- 3 cloves of garlic, minced
- 2 tablespoons fresh dill, finely chopped
- 1 tablespoon fresh lemon juice
- 2 tablespoons olive oil
- Salt and pepper to taste

Instructions:

1. Prepare the Cucumber: Start by grating the cucumber. Once grated, squeeze out as much moisture as possible. You can use a cheesecloth or a fine mesh strainer for this. The key is to get the cucumber as dry as possible to prevent a watery sauce.
2. Mix Ingredients: In a mixing bowl, combine the Greek yogurt, grated and drained cucumber, minced garlic, and chopped fresh dill. Stir until all the ingredients are well incorporated.
3. Add Flavors: Pour in the fresh lemon juice and olive oil. Mix well. The lemon juice adds a nice tang, while the olive oil gives a smooth texture.
4. Season: Add salt and pepper to taste. Adjust the seasoning according to your preference. Some people like their tzatziki with a stronger garlic flavor, while others prefer it more subtle.
5. Chill: Cover the bowl with plastic wrap and refrigerate for at least 2 hours. This allows the flavors to meld ogether beautifully.
6. Serve: Give it a quick stir before serving. Tzatziki can be served as a dip with pita bread, as a sauce for gyros, or as a refreshing side to grilled meats and vegetables.

Enjoy your homemade tzatziki sauce!

Mango Chutney Recipe

Easy Eats

Prep Time: 15 minutes
(not including cooking time)

Servings:
Makes multiple servings, exact number varies based on use.

Ingredients:

- 3 ripe mangoes, peeled and chopped (apples can be substituted)
- 1 medium onion, finely chopped
- 1 cup sugar
- 1 cup distilled white vinegar
- 1/2 cup raisins
- 2 garlic cloves, minced
- 1 tablespoon fresh ginger, grated
- 1 teaspoon mustard seeds
- 1/2 teaspoon red chili flakes (adjust to taste)
- 1/2 teaspoon ground cinnamon
- 1/4 teaspoon ground cloves
- Salt to taste

Instructions:

1. Combine Ingredients: In a large saucepan, combine the chopped mangoes, onion, sugar, and vinegar. Stir over medium heat until the sugar dissolves.
2. Add Spices and Raisins: Add the raisins, minced garlic, grated ginger, mustard seeds, red chili flakes, ground cinnamon, and ground cloves to the saucepan. Stir well to combine all the ingredients.
3. Simmer: Reduce the heat to low and let the mixture simmer for about 30-40 minutes, or until it thickens to a jam-like consistency. Stir occasionally to prevent sticking.
4. Season: Add salt to taste and adjust the seasoning as needed. If you prefer a sweeter chutney, you can add a bit more sugar.
5. Cool and Store: Remove the chutney from heat and let it cool to room temperature. Once cooled, transfer it to sterilized jars and seal.
6. Refrigerate: Store the mango chutney in the refrigerator. It will last for several weeks.

Enjoy your homemade mango chutney as a condiment with curries, grilled meats, or as a spread on sandwiches!

Spicy BBQ Sauce Recipe

Prep Time: 15 minutes
(not including cooking time)

Servings:
Makes about 1 1/2 cups, serving size varies based on use.

Ingredients:

- 1 cup ketchup
- 1/2 cup apple cider vinegar
- 1/2 cup brown sugar, packed
- 1/4 cup honey
- 1 tablespoon Worcestershire sauce
- 2 teaspoons smoked paprika
- 1 teaspoon garlic powder
- 1/2 teaspoon onion powder
- 1/2 teaspoon ground black pepper
- 1/2 teaspoon cayenne pepper (adjust for desired spiciness)
- 1/2 teaspoon dry mustard
- Salt to taste

Instructions:

1. In a medium saucepan, combine ketchup, apple cider vinegar, brown sugar, and honey. Stir over medium heat until well mixed.
2. Add Worcestershire sauce, smoked paprika, garlic powder, onion powder, black pepper, cayenne pepper, and dry mustard. Stir to combine.
3. Bring the mixture to a simmer over low heat. Allow it to cook for about 20-25 minutes, stirring occasionally, until the sauce thickens and the flavors meld together.
4. Taste and adjust seasoning with salt and more cayenne pepper if you prefer a spicier sauce.
5. Remove from heat and let the sauce cool down. If the sauce is too thick, you can thin it out with a little water or apple cider vinegar.
6. Store the BBQ sauce in an airtight container in the refrigerator for up to 2 weeks.

Enjoy your homemade spicy BBQ sauce with your favorite grilled meats or as a dipping sauce!

Classic Basil Pesto Recipe

Easy Eats

Prep Time:
10 minutes

Servings:
Makes about 1 cup, serving size varies based on use.

Ingredients:

- 2 cups fresh basil leaves, packed
- 1/2 cup freshly grated Parmesan-Reggiano or Romano cheese
- 1/2 cup extra virgin olive oil
- 1/3 cup pine nuts (can substitute walnuts)
- 3 medium-sized garlic cloves, minced
- Salt and freshly ground black pepper to taste

Instructions:

1. In a dry skillet over medium heat, lightly toast the pine nuts until they are slightly golden and fragrant. Be careful not to burn them. Remove from heat and let them cool.
2. Wash the basil leaves in cold water and thoroughly pat them dry with a paper towel.
3. In a food processor or blender, combine the basil leaves and pine nuts. Pulse a few times until roughly chopped.
4. Add the minced garlic and grated cheese to the basil mixture. While the processor is running, slowly pour in the olive oil in a steady stream. This will help to create a smooth and emulsified pesto.
5. Stop the processor and scrape down the sides with a spatula. Add salt and freshly ground black pepper to taste, then pulse again to mix.
6. If you prefer a smoother pesto, process for a few seconds more. For a chunkier texture, process less.
7. Transfer the pesto to a jar or container. If you're not using it immediately, pour a thin layer of olive oil over the top to prevent oxidation and maintain its vibrant green color. Seal and refrigerate.
8. Use your freshly made pesto with pasta, as a spread on sandwiches, in salad dressings, or as a marinade for meats and vegetables.

Enjoy your homemade pesto!

Easy Eats

Homemade Tartar Sauce

Prep Time:
10 minutes

Servings:
6-8 (makes about 1 cup)

Ingredients:

- 1 cup mayonnaise
- 1 tablespoon lemon juice
- 1 tablespoon dill pickle relish or chopped dill pickles
- 1 tablespoon capers, chopped (optional)
- 1 teaspoon Dijon mustard
- 1 teaspoon white onion, finely grated
- 1 tablespoon fresh dill, chopped (or 1 teaspoon dried dill)
- Salt and freshly ground black pepper to taste

Instructions:

1. In a medium bowl, combine the mayonnaise and lemon juice, stirring until well blended.
2. Stir in the pickle relish, capers (if using), and Dijon mustard.
3. Add the grated onion and fresh dill, and mix thoroughly.
4. Season with salt and pepper to taste.
5. Cover the bowl with plastic wrap and refrigerate for at least 30 minutes to allow the flavors to meld together.
6. Before serving, give the tartar sauce a final stir and adjust seasoning if necessary.

This tartar sauce is perfect for serving with fish, crab cakes, or as a dip for fried seafood. It's quick to make and can be easily adjusted to suit your taste—add more lemon juice for tanginess, or more relish for extra crunch and flavor. Enjoy your homemade tartar sauce!

Classic Remoulade Sauce

Prep Time:
10 minutes

Servings:
6-8 (makes about 1 cup)

Ingredients:

- 1 cup mayonnaise
- 2 tablespoons Dijon mustard
- 1 tablespoon lemon juice
- 1 tablespoon capers, drained and chopped
- 2 tablespoons parsley, finely chopped
- 1 green onion, finely chopped
- 1 clove garlic, minced
- 2 teaspoons horseradish
- 1 teaspoon paprika
- 1/4 teaspoon cayenne pepper
- Salt and freshly ground black pepper to taste

Instructions:

1. In a medium mixing bowl, combine the mayonnaise and Dijon mustard until smooth.
2. Stir in the lemon juice, capers, parsley, green onion, and minced garlic.
3. Add the horseradish, paprika, and cayenne pepper, and mix until all ingredients are well incorporated.
4. Season the remoulade sauce with salt and black pepper to your liking.
5. Cover the sauce with plastic wrap and refrigerate for at least 30 minutes to let the flavors come together.
6. Stir the sauce once more before serving and adjust any seasonings if necessary.

This remoulade is great served with seafood, especially crab cakes, fried fish, or as a spread on sandwiches. The slight kick from the horseradish and cayenne pepper adds depth to its flavor, making it a versatile condiment for a variety of dishes. Enjoy your homemade remoulade sauce!

Appetizers and Sides

Welcome to the "Appetizers and Sides" chapter, where the prelude to any meal turns into a festive spread worthy of celebration. Here, we delve into the heart of communal dining, perfecting the art of small plates that pack a punch of flavor. Whether you're gearing up for the Super Bowl, bringing people together for a casual get-together, or simply setting the stage for a grand meal, this chapter is your playbook for crowd-pleasing starters. From the classic crunch of nachos loaded with all the fixings to the delicate finesse of crab cakes served with a tangy remoulade, we've curated a collection that will have your guests cheering for more. These recipes are designed not only to satisfy cravings but also to bring people together, sharing in the universal language of good food. So, gather your ingredients, and let's kick off the festivities with appetizers and sides that will score big at any gathering!

Buffalo Chicken Wings Recipe with Oven and Air Fryer Options

Prep Time:
10 minutes

Servings:
6-8 (makes about 1 cup)

Ingredients:

- 2 lbs chicken wings, split at joints, tips discarded
- 1 tbsp baking powder (aluminum-free)
- 1 tsp garlic powder
- Salt and pepper to taste
- 1/2 cup buffalo wing sauce (store-bought or homemade)
- 2 tbsp unsalted butter, melted
- 1 tbsp honey (optional, for a slight sweetness)

Instructions:

1. For the Oven:
- Preheat your oven to 425 degrees F (220 degrees C). Place a rack on a baking sheet and lightly grease it to prevent sticking.
- Pat the chicken wings dry with paper towels to remove excess moisture. This will help to get them crispy.
- In a bowl, toss the wings with baking powder, garlic powder, salt, and pepper until they are evenly coated.
- Arrange the wings on the prepared rack in a single layer.
- Bake in the preheated oven for about 45-50 minutes, or until they are golden brown and crisp, turning them halfway through the baking time.

2. For the Air Fryer:
- Preheat the air fryer to 380 degrees F (190 degrees C) if your air fryer requires preheating.
- Prepare the wings with the same dry mixture as above.
- Place the wings in the air fryer basket in a single layer, ensuring they are not touching for proper air circulation.
- Cook for about 22-25 minutes, shaking the basket or flipping the wings halfway through, until they are crisp and golden brown.

3. For the Buffalo Sauce:
- While the wings are cooking, prepare the buffalo sauce by combining buffalo wing sauce, melted butter, and honey (if using) in a saucepan. Heat over low heat until the mixture is well combined and slightly thickened.
- Once the wings are cooked, place them in a large bowl.
- Pour the buffalo sauce over the wings and toss to coat them evenly.

4. Serving:
- Serve the buffalo wings hot with celery sticks and carrot sticks on the side.
- Offer blue cheese dressing or ranch dressing for dipping.

Enjoy your spicy and tangy buffalo chicken wings, perfect for game day, gatherings, or a flavorful dinner!

Easy Eats

Potato Skins Recipe

Prep Time:
1 hour 30 minutes

Servings:
6

Ingredients:

- 6 medium russet potatoes, scrubbed and dried
- 2 tablespoons olive oil
- Salt and ground black pepper, to taste
- 1 cup shredded cheddar cheese
- 6 strips of bacon, cooked and crumbled
- 1/3 cup sour cream
- 2 green onions, thinly sliced
- Optional: 1/4 cup chopped fresh chives, for garnish

Instructions:

1. Preheat your oven to 400 degrees F (200 degrees C).
2. Pierce the potatoes a few times with a fork and bake them directly on the oven rack for about 1 hour, or until they are tender when pierced with a fork. Remove from the oven and let them cool slightly.
3. Once the potatoes are cool enough to handle, cut them in half length-wise. Scoop out most of the flesh, leaving about 1/4 inch of potato on the skin. (Reserve the scooped potato for another use, like mashed potatoes or potato soup.)
4. Increase the oven temperature to 450 degrees F (230 degrees C).
5. Brush both the inside and outside of the potato skins with olive oil. Sprinkle the insides with salt and pepper to taste.
6. Place the potato skins skin-side up on a baking sheet and bake for about 10 minutes. Flip the skins over and bake for another 5 to 10 minutes, or until the edges are crispy and starting to brown.
7. Remove the skins from the oven. Sprinkle the cheddar cheese evenly among the skins, and top with the crumbled bacon.
8. Return the potato skins to the oven and bake for an additional 2 to 3 minutes, or until the cheese is melted and bubbly.
9. Remove the potato skins from the oven. Dollop sour cream on each skin and sprinkle with sliced green onions and optional chives.
10. Serve hot as an appetizer or a side dish. Enjoy your homemade potato skins with additional sour cream or your favorite dipping sauce on the side.

Note:

Save the inside potato you scooped for mashed potatoes for dinner.

Egg Rolls Recipe

Prep Time:
30 minutes

Servings:
4-6

Ingredients:

- 1 lb ground pork (or chicken)
- 1 cup shredded cabbage
- 1/2 cup shredded carrots
- 2 cloves garlic, minced
- 1 tablespoon soy sauce
- 1 teaspoon sesame oil
- Egg roll wrappers
- Vegetable oil for frying

Instructions:

1. In a skillet, cook the ground pork over medium heat until no longer pink. Drain excess fat.
2. Add cabbage, carrots, and garlic to the skillet. Cook until vegetables are tender.
3. Appetizers and Sides
4. Stir in soy sauce and sesame oil. Remove from heat.
5. Place a spoonful of the filling onto each egg roll wrapper. Fold according to package instructions, sealing the edges with a bit of water.
6. Heat oil in a deep pan. Fry the egg rolls until golden brown on all sides. Drain on paper towels.
7. Alternatively, you can use an Air Fryer at 410 degrees for 10-12 minutes or until crispy.

Easy Eats

Classic Nachos

Prep Time:

25 minutes

Servings:
4-6

Ingredients:

- 1 bag of tortilla chips
- 1 cup of shredded cheddar cheese
- 1 cup of Monterey Jack cheese
- 1 (15-ounce) can of black beans, drained and rinsed
- 1 large tomato, diced
- 1/4 cup of sliced jalapeños (pickled or fresh)
- 1/4 cup of red onion, diced
- 1/4 cup of black olives, sliced (optional)
- 1/4 cup of fresh cilantro, chopped
- 1 ripe avocado, diced or guacamole
- Sour cream, for serving
- Salsa, for serving

Instructions:

1. Preheat Oven: Preheat your oven to 375°F (190°C).
2. Layer the Chips and Cheese: On an ovenproof platter or baking sheet, spread out half the tortilla chips and sprinkle with half of the cheddar and Monterey Jack cheeses, followed by half of the black beans. Repeat with another layer of chips, cheese, and beans.
3. Add Toppings: Scatter the diced tomato, sliced jalapeños, red onion, and black olives over the top.
4. Bake: Place the nachos in the preheated oven and bake for 10-15 minutes, or until the cheese is melted and bubbly.
5. Add Final Toppings: Once the nachos are baked, remove them from the oven and immediately top with the fresh cilantro and diced avocado or dollops of guacamole.
6. Serve: Serve the nachos hot with sides of sour cream and salsa.

For an extra touch, you can add cooked ground beef, shredded chicken, or pulled pork on top of the beans before adding the second layer of chips and cheese. Enjoy your homemade classic nachos!

Artichoke Spinach Dip Recipe

Prep Time:
35 minutes

Servings:
8

Ingredients:

- 1 cup chopped spinach (fresh or thawed from frozen)
- 1 1/2 cups chopped canned artichoke hearts
- 6 ounces cream cheese, softened
- 1/4 cup sour cream
- 1/4 cup mayonnaise
- 1 clove garlic, minced
- 1/2 cup grated Parmesan cheese
- 1/2 cup shredded mozzarella cheese
- 1/2 teaspoon salt
- 1/4 teaspoon black pepper
- 1/4 teaspoon paprika (optional for smoky flavor)
- 1 tablespoon lemon juice
- 1/2 teaspoon onion powder

Instructions:

1. Preheat Oven: Preheat your oven to 375°F (190°C).
2. Prepare Spinach and Artichokes: If using frozen spinach, squeeze out the excess moisture. Roughly chop the artichoke hearts.
3. Mix the Ingredients: In a mixing bowl, combine the cream cheese, sour cream, mayonnaise, minced garlic, Parmesan cheese, half of the shredded mozzarella, salt, pepper, paprika, lemon juice, and onion powder. Mix until well blended.
4. Add Vegetables: Stir in the chopped spinach and artichoke hearts until they are evenly distributed throughout the mixture.
5. Transfer to Baking Dish: Spread the mixture into an 8-inch baking dish or pie plate.
6. Top with Cheese: Sprinkle the remaining mozzarella cheese on top of the mixture.
7. Bake: Place the dish in the preheated oven and bake for 20-25 minutes, or until the dip is hot and the cheese is melted and lightly browned on top.
8. Serve: Remove the dip from the oven and let it cool for a few minutes. Serve warm with tortilla chips, sliced baguette, or crudité.

For a richer flavor, you can add 1/2 cup of grated Gruyère or Fontina cheese to the mixture. You can also add a pinch of red pepper flakes for a spicy kick. Enjoy your homemade artichoke spinach dip!

Easy Eats

Classic 7-Layer Dip Recipe

Prep Time:
15 minutes (plus chilling time)

Servings:
8

Ingredients:

- 1 (16-ounce) can refried beans
- 1 tablespoon taco seasoning
- 1 cup guacamole (homemade or store-bought)
- 1 cup sour cream
- 1 cup salsa (choose your preferred level of spiciness)
- 1 cup shredded cheddar cheese or Mexican blend cheese
- 1/2 cup chopped black olives
- 1/2 cup chopped tomatoes
- 1/2 cup sliced green onions
- 1/4 cup sliced jalapeños (optional for extra heat)
- Fresh cilantro for garnish (optional)

Instructions:

1. Prepare the Refried Beans: In a bowl, mix the refried beans with the taco seasoning until well combined. Spread the mixture evenly on the bottom of a 9x13 inch serving dish or a large pie plate.
2. Layer the Guacamole: Carefully spread the guacamole over the refried beans, taking care not to mix the layers.
3. Add the Sour Cream: Spread the sour cream over the guacamole layer.
4. Layer the Salsa: Gently spoon the salsa over the sour cream and spread it out evenly.
5. Add the Cheese: Sprinkle the shredded cheese over the salsa, covering it completely.
6. Top with Olives and Tomatoes: Scatter the chopped black olives and Appetizers and Sides tomatoes over the cheese layer.
7. Garnish: Add the sliced green onions and, if using, the jalapeños on top. Garnish with fresh cilantro leaves if desired.
8. Chill: Cover the dish with plastic wrap and chill in the refrigerator for at least 1 hour to allow the flavors to meld.
9. Serve: Serve the 7-layer dip with tortilla chips, pita chips, or vegetable sticks for dipping.

For a personalized touch, you can add a layer of cooked and crumbled ground beef or shredded chicken between the refried beans and guacamole layers. Also, feel free to adjust the layers with additional toppings like corn, diced bell peppers, or a drizzle of hot sauce. Enjoy your colorful and flavorful classic 7-layer dip!

Classic Crab Cake Appetizer

Prep Time: 20 minutes | Cooking Time: 10 minutes | Total Time: 30 minutes

Servings: 4-6

Ingredients:

- 1 pound lump crab meat, picked over for shells
- 1/2 cup breadcrumbs or cracker crumbs
- 1/4 cup mayonnaise
- 1 large egg
- 1 tablespoon Dijon mustard
- 1 tablespoon Worcestershire sauce
- 1/2 teaspoon hot sauce
- 1/4 cup finely chopped fresh parsley
- 2 tablespoons finely chopped green onions
- 1 teaspoon Old Bay seasoning
- Salt and freshly ground black pepper to taste
- 1/4 cup vegetable oil or butter for frying For Serving:
- Lemon wedges
- Tartar sauce or remoulade

Instructions:

1. In a large mixing bowl, combine the crab meat and breadcrumbs.
2. In a separate small bowl, whisk together mayonnaise, egg, Dijon mustard, Worcestershire sauce, hot sauce, parsley, green onions, and Old Bay seasoning. Season with salt and pepper.
3. Pour the wet mixture over the crab mixture and gently fold together, being careful not to break up the crab meat too much.
4. Shape the mixture into small patties, about 2 inches wide and 1/2 inch thick.
5. Heat oil or butter in a large skillet over medium-high heat.
6. Once the oil is hot, carefully add the crab cakes and fry for about 3-4 minutes on each side, or until they are golden brown and crispy.
7. Remove from the skillet and drain on paper towels to remove any excess oil.
8. Serve the crab cakes warm with lemon wedges and tartar sauce or remoulade on the side for dipping.

Enjoy your crab cake appetizers as a delightful start to any meal or as a part of a seafood feast!

Easy Eats

Classic Burger Slider

Prep Time: 30 minutes |
Cooking Time: 10 minutes

Servings:
12 sliders

Ingredients:

- 1 pound ground beef (80/20 blend for best flavor)
- Salt and freshly ground black pepper to taste
- 1 package (12 count) Hawaiian sweet rolls
- 6 slices of cheese (cheddar or American), quartered
- Lettuce leaves, torn to bun size
- 1 tomato, sliced into 12 slices
- 1 small onion, thinly sliced
- Ketchup, mustard, and mayonnaise for serving

Instructions:

1. Preheat your grill or stovetop griddle to medium-high heat.
2. Divide the ground beef into 12 equal portions and form into small patties, slightly larger than your buns.
3. Season both sides of the patties with salt and pepper.
4. Grill the patties for about 2-3 minutes per side for medium-rare, or until they reach your desired doneness.
5. In the last minute of cooking, place a quarter slice of cheese on each patty to melt.
6. Assemble the sliders on the buns with lettuce, tomato, onion, and your choice of condiments.
7. Serve immediately and enjoy!

Buffalo Chicken Slider

Prep Time: 20 minutes |
Cooking Time: 20 minutes

Servings:
12 sliders

Ingredients:

- 2 cups shredded cooked chicken
- 1/2 cup buffalo sauce
- 1 package (12 count) Hawaiian sweet rolls
- 1/2 cup ranch or blue cheese dressing
- 1 stalk celery, thinly sliced
- 1/2 cup crumbled blue cheese

Instructions:

1. In a bowl, mix the shredded chicken with buffalo sauce until well coated.
2. Preheat your oven to 350°F (175°C).
3. Place the bottom half of the slider buns on a baking sheet.
4. Divide the buffalo chicken mixture evenly among the buns.
5. Drizzle ranch or blue cheese dressing over the chicken.
6. Sprinkle with sliced celery and crumbled blue cheese.
7. Cover with the top halves of the slider buns.
8. Bake in the oven for 10-15 minutes until everything is heated through and the buns are slightly crispy.
9. Serve hot and enjoy the kick of these spicy sliders!

Easy Eats

BBQ Chicken Slider

Prep Time: 20 minutes | Cooking Time: 25 minutes

Servings: 12 sliders

Ingredients:

- 1 package (12 count) Hawaiian sweet rolls
- 2 cups cooked chicken breast, shredded
- 3/4 cup BBQ sauce, plus extra for drizzling
- 1/2 red onion, thinly sliced
- 6 slices of cheddar cheese, cut in half
- 1/4 cup melted butter
- 1 teaspoon smoked paprika (optional)
- 1 tablespoon chopped parsley or cilantro for garnish (optional)

Instructions:

1. Preheat your oven to 350°F (175°C).
2. Keep the Hawaiian rolls connected to each other and slice the entire block horizontally in half to create a top and bottom layer.
3. Place the bottom layer of the Hawaiian rolls in a greased baking dish.
4. In a mixing bowl, toss the shredded chicken with the BBQ sauce until it's well coated.
5. Spread the BBQ chicken mixture evenly over the bottom layer of the Hawaiian rolls in the baking dish.
6. Distribute the sliced red onions over the chicken.
7. Lay the cheddar cheese halves over the onions, covering the chicken mixture.
8. Place the top layer of the Hawaiian rolls onto the cheese.
9. In a small bowl, mix the melted butter with smoked paprika if using, then brush the mixture over the top of the rolls.
10. Cover the baking dish with aluminum foil and bake in the preheated oven for 20 minutes.
11. Remove the foil and bake for another 5 minutes or until the tops of the rolls are slightly crispy and golden brown.
12. Take the sliders out of the oven, let them rest for a few minutes, and then cut them into individual sliders using the roll lines as a guide.
13. Garnish with chopped parsley or cilantro, drizzle with a little more BBQ sauce if desired, and serve warm.

These BBQ chicken sliders are the perfect combination of sweet and tangy flavors, all packed into a delightful Hawaiian roll. They are ideal for parties, family gatherings, or as a tasty treat during game day festivities. Enjoy

Enjoy these delicious sliders at your next party or gathering—they're guaranteed to be a hit!

Easy Eats

Homemade Macaroni and Cheese

Prep Time:

45 minutes

Servings:

8

Ingredients:

- 1 pound elbow macaroni
- 1/4 cup unsalted butter
- 1/4 cup all-purpose flour
- 3 cups whole milk
- 1 cup heavy cream
- 4 cups shredded sharp cheddar cheese
- 1 cup shredded Gruyère cheese (or additional cheddar cheese)
- 1 teaspoon dry mustard powder
- 1/2 teaspoon smoked paprika
- Salt and pepper to taste
- 1/2 teaspoon garlic powder (optional)
- Bread crumbs or crushed crackers for topping (optional)
- Fresh parsley, chopped for garnish (optional)

Instructions:

1. Cook the Pasta:
- Bring a large pot of salted water to a boil.
- Add the elbow macaroni and cook according to package instructions until al dente.
- Drain the macaroni and set aside.
2. Make the Roux:
- In the same pot or a large saucepan, melt the butter over medium heat.
- Sprinkle in the flour and whisk constantly for about 1 minute to cook out the raw flour taste.
3. Develop the Sauce:
- Gradually pour in the milk and heavy cream, whisking constantly to prevent any lumps from forming.
- Continue to whisk the mixture until it thickens to the consistency of a creamy sauce, which may take about 5-7 minutes.
4. Add Seasoning:
- Stir in the dry mustard powder, smoked paprika, garlic powder (if using), and salt and pepper to taste.
5. Cheese Please:
- Reduce the heat to low and begin adding the shredded cheeses, a handful at a time, stirring well after each addition until the cheese is fully melted and the sauce is smooth.
6. Combine Pasta and Cheese Sauce:
- Add the cooked macaroni to the cheese sauce and stir until the pasta is completely coated.
7. Bake (Optional):
- f you prefer baked macaroni and cheese, preheat your oven to 350°F (175°C).
- Transfer the macaroni and cheese to a greased baking dish.
- Top with bread crumbs or crushed crackers if desired for a crunchy topping.
- Bake for 20-25 minutes, or until the topping is golden and the edges are bubbly.
8. Garnish and Serve:
- Optionally, sprinkle with fresh chopped parsley for color and freshness.
- Serve the macaroni and cheese hot as a satisfying main dish or a hearty side.
- Making a roux-based cheese sauce ensures your macaroni and cheese will be creamy and free of clumps.
- Feel free to mix and match different types of cheese according to your preference. Just make sure they are good melting cheeses.
- Leftovers can be stored in the refrigerator and are often even tastier the next day as the flavors meld together overnight.

Easy Eats

Homemade Garlic Naan Recipe

Prep Time: 1 hour 30 minutes
(including rise time)

Servings:
16

Ingredients:

- 2 cups all-purpose flour
- 1 tsp instant yeast
- 1 tsp sugar
- 1/2 tsp salt
- 3/4 cup warm water
- 1/4 cup plain yogurt
- 2 tbsp olive oil
- 4 cloves garlic, finely minced
- 2 tbsp fresh cilantro, chopped
- Butter, for brushing

Instructions:

1. In a large mixing bowl, combine flour, instant yeast, sugar, and salt.
2. Make a well in the center of the dry ingredients and add warm water, yogurt, and olive oil. Mix until a soft dough forms. If the dough is too sticky, add a bit more flour. If too dry, add a little more water.
3. Turn the dough out onto a floured surface and knead for about 5-7 minutes, until smooth and elastic.
4. Place the dough in a greased bowl, cover with a clean kitchen towel, and let it rise in a warm place for about 1 hour, or until doubled in size.
5. Once risen, punch down the dough and divide it into 6 equal portions. Roll each portion into a ball.
6. Heat a skillet or griddle over medium-high heat. While it's heating, roll out one ball of dough into an oval shape, about 1/8 inch thick.
7. Before placing the naan on the skillet, sprinkle one side with minced garlic and press it lightly into the dough.
8. Place the naan, garlic side up, on the hot skillet. Cook until bubbles form on the surface, then flip it over and cook until the other side is golden and puffed.
9. Remove the naan from the skillet, brush with butter, and sprinkle with chopped cilantro.
10. Repeat with the remaining dough.
11. Serve warm and enjoy your homemade garlic naan with your favorite dishes!

This homemade garlic naan is perfect for scooping up curries, dips, or as a delicious side to any meal. Enjoy the process of making it and the wonderful flavors it brings to your table.

Soups and Salads

Welcome to the warm and welcoming world of "Soups and Salads," a chapter dedicated to the harmonious blend of hearty comfort and refreshing crispness. Here, we dive into the soul-soothing depths of rich, creamy clam chowder, a maritime marvel that encapsulates the essence of coastal cuisine. Alongside, we toss up the classic Cobb salad, a symphony of textures and flavors that promises a satisfying crunch with every forkful. Whether you're wrapped in a blanket on a chilly evening or enjoying the shade on a sunny afternoon, this collection brings you an array of recipes that stand as meals in their own right. From broths brimming with nourishment to salads layered with a bounty of fresh produce, proteins, and dressings, each recipe is a tribute to the simple, unadulterated pleasure of good food. So, grab your spoon or your salad tongs, and let's embark on a culinary journey that celebrates the best of both worlds.

Easy Eats

Homestyle Chicken Noodle Soup

Prep Time: 15 minutes | Cooking Time: 30 minutes | Total Time: 45 minutes

Servings: 6

Ingredients:

- 2 tablespoons olive oil
- 1 large onion, chopped
- 3 carrots, peeled and sliced
- 3 celery stalks, sliced
- 2 cloves garlic, minced
- 8 cups chicken broth
- 2 bay leaves
- 1 teaspoon dried thyme or 2 sprigs fresh thyme
- Salt and pepper, to taste
- 2 cups cooked chicken, shredded (rotisserie chicken works well)
- 2 cups egg noodles
- Fresh parsley, chopped, for garnish

Instructions:

1. Sauté Vegetables: Heat olive oil in a pot over medium heat. Sauté onion, carrots, and celery for 5 minutes until they begin to soften.
2. Add Garlic: Include garlic and sauté for another minute until fragrant.
3. Pour in Broth: Add broth, bay leaves, and thyme to the pot. Season with salt and pepper.
4. Simmer: Bring to a boil, then lower the heat and simmer for 15 minutes.
5. Add Chicken and Noodles: Incorporate the chicken and noodles into the soup, simmering for 10 more minutes until noodles are tender.
6. Discard Bay Leaves: Remove the bay leaves.
7. Adjust Seasonings: Taste and adjust for salt and pepper.
8. Serve: Serve the soup in bowls, garnished with fresh parsley.

This chicken noodle soup is the epitome of comfort food, easy to make and filled with the goodness of vegetables, tender chicken, and noodles. It's a perfect meal to enjoy on a cold day or when you need a little comfort. Enjoy your meal!

Easy Eats

Hearty Beef Minestrone Soup

Prep Time: 20 minutes | Cooking Time: 30 minutes | Total Time: 50 minutes

Servings: 6-8

Ingredients:

- 1 tablespoon olive oil
- 1 pound lean beef stew meat, cut into small cubes
- 1 large onion, chopped
- 2 cloves garlic, minced
- 2 carrots, peeled and diced
- 2 stalks celery, diced
- 1 zucchini, diced
- 1 cup green beans, trimmed and cut into 1-inch pieces
- 1 can (14.5 ounces) diced tomatoes, undrained
- 6 cups beef broth
- 1 can (15 ounces) kidney beans, drained and rinsed
- 1 can (15 ounces) cannellini beans, drained and rinsed
- 1 teaspoon dried basil
- 1 teaspoon dried oregano
- Salt and freshly ground black pepper, to taste
- 1 cup small pasta (such as ditalini or elbow macaroni)
- 2 cups fresh spinach, roughly chopped
- Grated Parmesan cheese, for serving

Instructions:

1. Brown the Beef: Heat olive oil in a pot over medium-high heat. Brown beef for 5-7 minutes, then set aside.
2. Sauté Vegetables: In the same pot, sauté onion, garlic, carrots, and celery for 5 minutes.
3. Add Zucchini and Green Beans: Cook for 3 more minutes.
4. Add Tomatoes and Broth: Bring to a boil.
5. Return Beef to Pot: Simmer for about 15 minutes.
6. Add Beans and Seasonings: Stir and season.
7. dd Pasta: Cook until al dente.
8. Add Spinach: Cook until wilted, about 2 minutes.
9. Serve: Garnish with Parmesan cheese and serve hot.

This robust Beef Minestrone soup is filled with tender beef, hearty vegetables, and beans, all simmered to perfection. It's a filling and nutritious meal that's perfect for any day of the week. Enjoy with a sprinkle of Parmesan on top for added flavor!

Easy Eats

Hearty Italian Wedding Soup

Prep Time: 20 minutes | Cooking Time: 30 minutes | Total Time: 1 hour

Servings: 6-8

Ingredients:

For the Meatballs:

- 1/2 pound ground beef
- 1/2 pound ground pork
- 1/3 cup breadcrumbs
- 1/4 cup grated Parmesan cheese
- 2 cloves garlic, minced
- 1 large egg
- 1 teaspoon dried basil
- 1 teaspoon dried oregano
- Salt and freshly ground black pepper, to taste For the Soup:
- 2 tablespoons olive oil
- 1 cup chopped onion
- 1 cup diced carrots
- 1 cup diced celery
- 8 cups chicken broth
- 1 cup acini di pepe pasta or small pasta of your choice
- 1 teaspoon dried basil
- 1 teaspoon dried oregano
- Salt and freshly ground black pepper, to taste
- 4 cups fresh spinach, roughly chopped
- Grated Parmesan cheese, for serving

Instructions:

1. Preheat Oven & Prepare Baking Sheet: Preheat your oven to 350°F (175°C). Line a baking sheet with parchment paper.
2. Make Meatballs: Combine all meatball ingredients in a large bowl. Form into 1-inch diameter balls and place on the baking sheet.
3. Bake Meatballs: Bake for 20 minutes, or until cooked and slightly browned.
4. Cook Vegetables: Heat olive oil in a pot over medium heat. Sauté onion,
5. carrots, and celery until softened, about 5-7 minutes.
6. Add Broth and Seasonings: Pour in chicken broth and add seasonings. Bring to a boil.
7. Add Pasta: Stir in pasta and cook until al dente.
8. Add Meatballs: Add the baked meatballs to the soup and simmer for a few minutes.
9. Add Spinach: Mix in spinach and cook until wilted, about 2 minutes.
10. Serve: Ladle soup into bowls, top with grated Parmesan cheese, and serve hot.

This Italian Wedding Soup is a flavorful, nourishing meal that combines homemade meatballs and fresh vegetables in a rich broth, perfect for a comforting dinner. Enjoy!

Easy Eats

Traditional Clam Chowder

Prep Time: 20 minutes | Cooking Time: 30 minutes | Total Time: 50 minutes

Servings: 6-8

Ingredients:

- 4 cups chopped clams, with juice reserved
- 4 cups fish stock or clam juice
- 3 slices bacon, chopped
- 1 large onion, finely chopped
- 2 celery stalks, finely chopped
- 3 medium potatoes, peeled and diced
- 1 bay leaf
- 1 teaspoon dried thyme
- 1/2 cup butter
- 1/2 cup all-purpose flour
- 2 cups heavy cream
- Salt and freshly ground black pepper, to taste
- Fresh parsley, chopped, for garnish

Instructions:

1. Prepare Clams: Drain the clams, reserving the juice. Combine with enough fish stock or clam juice to total 4 cups.
2. Cook Bacon: Over medium heat, cook the bacon in a large pot until crisp. Remove the bacon and set it aside, leaving the fat in the pot.
3. Sauté Vegetables: In the bacon fat, sauté the onion and celery until soft, about 5 minutes.
4. Add Potatoes and Herbs: Stir in the potatoes, bay leaf, and thyme.
5. Pour in Liquid: Add the clam juice and fish stock mixture. Bring to a boil, then simmer until the potatoes are tender, roughly 15 minutes.
6. Make Roux: In a separate pan, melt butter, whisk in flour, and cook for a couple of minutes to create a roux.
7. Combine Roux and Soup: Gradually incorporate the roux into the soup to thicken it, cooking for a few minutes.
8. Add Cream and Clams: Lower the heat, add cream and clams, and warm through for about 5 minutes without boiling.
9. Season: Remove the bay leaf and season with salt and pepper.
10. Serve: Serve the chowder garnished with crispy bacon and parsley.

This clam chowder is a comforting, creamy delight, ideal for warming up on cool days or whenever you crave a rich, satisfying soup. Enjoy your homemade clam chowder with a side of oyster crackers or fresh bread for the perfect meal!

Hearty Split Pea Soup

Prep Time: 10 minutes | Cooking Time: 1 to 1.5 hours | Total Time: 1 hour 20 minutes

Servings: 6-8

Ingredients:

- 2 tablespoons olive oil
- 1 large onion, chopped
- 2 carrots, peeled and diced
- 2 celery stalks, diced
- 2 cloves garlic, minced
- 1 pound dried split peas, rinsed and sorted
- 8 cups chicken or vegetable broth
- 1 bay leaf
- 1 teaspoon dried thyme
- Salt and pepper, to taste
- Optional: 1 ham hock or smoked turkey leg (for non-vegetarian version)

Instructions:

1. Prepare the Vegetables: Heat the olive oil in a large pot over medium heat. Add the onion, carrots, and celery. Sauté for about 5 minutes until they begin to soften.
2. Add Garlic: Incorporate the minced garlic into the pot and continue to sauté for another minute until it's fragrant.
3. Add Split Peas: Add the split peas to the pot, mixing them with the sautéed vegetables.
4. Add Broth and Seasonings: Pour in the broth, and add the bay leaf and dried thyme. Season with salt and pepper to your liking. If choosing the non-vegetarian option, add the ham hock or smoked turkey leg now.
5. Simmer: Bring the soup to a boil, then lower the heat, cover, and let it simmer for 1 to 1.5 hours, stirring occasionally. The soup is ready when the split peas are soft and the soup has thickened to your preference.
6. Final Touches: Remove the bay leaf and, if used, the meat. Shred the meat and return it to the pot. If the soup is too thick, adjust the consistency by adding more broth or water.
7. Adjust Seasonings: Do a final taste test and tweak the salt and pepper as needed.
8. Serve: Ladle the hot soup into bowls and serve with a side of crusty bread or croutons for added texture.

This split pea soup is a classic, comforting dish that's perfect for a wholesome dinner, especially on those cooler evenings. Enjoy!

Easy Eats

Garden Salad Recipe

Prep Time:
20 minutes

Servings:
4-6

Ingredients:

- 4 cups mixed greens (lettuce, spinach, arugula)
- 1 cup cherry tomatoes, halved
- 1 cucumber, sliced
- 1 bell pepper, diced (any color)
- 1/2 red onion, thinly sliced
- 1/2 cup shredded carrots
- 1/4 cup radishes, thinly sliced
- 1/4 cup sunflower seeds or sliced almonds
- Optional: crumbled feta or goat cheese
- Your choice of salad dressing (Italian, vinaigrette, or ranch)

Instructions:

1. Prepare the Greens:
- Wash and dry the mixed greens thoroughly. Tear or cut any large leaves into bite-sized pieces.

2. Chop Vegetables:
- Prepare the cherry tomatoes, cucumber, bell pepper, red onion, shredded carrots, and radishes by washing, drying, and then slicing or dicing them.

3. Assemble the Salad:
- In a large salad bowl, combine the mixed greens with the prepared vegetables.

4. Add Seeds or Nuts:
- Sprinkle the sunflower seeds or sliced almonds over the salad for added crunch.

5. Add Cheese (Optional):
- If using, sprinkle crumbled feta or goat cheese over the salad for extra flavor.

6. Dress the Salad:
- Right before serving, drizzle your choice of salad dressing over the garden salad and toss gently to combine.

7. Serve:
- Serve the garden salad immediately as a fresh and vibrant side dish or light meal.

Enjoy your colorful and nutritious garden salad, a delightful blend of fresh vegetables and greens!

Spinach Strawberry Salad with Feta and Candied Pecans

Prep Time:
20 minutes

Servings:
4-6

Ingredients:

- 4 cups fresh baby spinach
- 1 cup strawberries, hulled and sliced
- 1/2 cup feta cheese, crumbled
- 1/2 cup candied pecans (recipe below)
- 1/4 cup red onion, thinly sliced
- 2 tablespoons balsamic vinegar
- 1/4 cup extra virgin olive oil
- 1 tablespoon honey
- Salt and pepper, to taste

For Candied Pecans:

- 1 cup pecan halves
- 2 tablespoons brown sugar
- 1 tablespoon butter
- Pinch of salt

Instructions:

1. Make the Candied Pecans:
- In a skillet over medium heat, melt the butter. Add the brown sugar and stir until dissolved.
- Add the pecans and a pinch of salt. Cook, stirring frequently, for about 5 minutes until the pecans are well coated and fragrant. Spread them on parchment paper to cool.

2. Prepare the Salad:
- In a large salad bowl, combine the baby spinach, sliced strawberries, and thinly sliced red onion.

3. Make the Dressing:
- In a small bowl, whisk together the balsamic vinegar, olive oil, and honey. Season with salt and pepper to taste.

4. Assemble the Salad:
- Drizzle the dressing over the spinach and strawberry mixture. Toss gently to coat.

5. Add the Toppings:
- Sprinkle the crumbled feta cheese and candied pecans over the salad.

6. Serve:
- Serve immediately for the freshest taste. This salad is perfect as a light lunch or as a side dish for a summer meal.

Enjoy the delightful combination of sweet strawberries, creamy feta, and crunchy candied pecans in this refreshing spinach salad!

Easy Eats

Classic Caesar Salad

Prep Time:
20 minutes

Servings:
4-6

Ingredients:

- 2 heads of romaine lettuce, washed and dried
- 3/4 cup croutons (homemade or store-bought)
- 1/2 cup freshly grated Parmesan cheese
- 2 garlic cloves, minced
- 2 anchovy fillets, finely chopped (optional)
- 1 egg yolk (or 1 tablespoon mayonnaise for a raw egg-free version)
- 1 tablespoon Dijon mustard
- 2 tablespoons fresh lemon juice
- 1/2 cup extra virgin olive oil
- Salt and freshly ground black pepper, to taste

Instructions:

1. Prepare the Lettuce: Tear the romaine lettuce into bite-sized pieces and place them in a large salad bowl. This step should take about 5 minutes.
2. Make the Dressing: In a small bowl, combine the minced garlic, anchovy fillets (if using), egg yolk, and Dijon mustard. Whisk together until well combined, which should take about 3 minutes. Add the lemon juice and whisk again. Gradually whisk in the olive oil until the dressing is emulsified. Season with salt and pepper to taste. This part of the preparation should take around 7 minutes.
3. Dress the Salad: Drizzle the dressing over the romaine lettuce in the salad bowl. Toss gently to ensure all the leaves are coated with the dressing, which should take about 2 minutes.
4. Add Croutons and Cheese: Sprinkle the croutons and freshly grated Parmesan cheese over the dressed lettuce. Toss lightly again, for roughly 1 minute.
5. Serve: Serve the Caesar salad immediately, optionally garnished with additional Parmesan cheese or lemon wedges for added zest.

Enjoy this classic Caesar salad as a refreshing starter or a light yet satisfying meal. The combination of crisp romaine, creamy dressing, and the crunch of croutons is always a crowd-pleaser!

Wedge Salad Recipe

Prep Time:
20 minutes

Servings:
4

Iceberg Lettuce Wedge Salad
Ingredients:

- 1 head of iceberg lettuce
- 1 cup cherry tomatoes, halved
- 1/2 cup blue cheese, crumbled
- 6 slices of bacon
- 1/2 red onion, thinly sliced
- 1/2 cup blue cheese dressing
- Freshly ground black pepper
- Optional: Fresh chives or parsley for garnish

Instructions:

1. Prepare the Lettuce: Rinse the iceberg lettuce and pat it dry with paper towels. Remove any wilted or discolored outer leaves. Cut the head of lettuce into 4 equal wedges. This should take about 5 minutes.
2. Cook the Bacon: In a skillet over medium heat, cook the bacon slices until crispy, which should take about 10 minutes. Then place them on a paper towel to drain and cool. Once cooled, crumble the bacon into small pieces.
3. Assemble the Salad: Place each lettuce wedge on a plate. Drizzle each wedge generously with blue cheese dressing. This step should take about 2 minutes.
4. Add Toppings: Sprinkle the crumbled bacon, blue cheese, sliced red onions, and cherry tomatoes over each wedge. This should take about 3 minutes.
5. Season: Add freshly ground black pepper to taste. Optionally, garnish with chopped fresh chives or parsley for added color and flavor. The seasoning and garnishing should take about 1 minute.
6. Serve: Present the wedge salad immediately to ensure the freshness and crunch of the lettuce with a balanced distribution of toppings and dressing.

This wedge salad is a classic starter that's as elegant as it is easy to prepare. The crispness of the iceberg lettuce combined with the rich flavors of blue cheese and bacon make for a delightful dish. Enjoy your meal!

Classic Coleslaw

Prep Time:
15 minutes
(plus at least 1 hour chilling time)

Servings:
6-8

Ingredients:

- 1 head of green cabbage, finely shredded
- 2 large carrots, grated
- 1 small onion, finely chopped (optional)
- 1/2 cup mayonnaise
- 2 tablespoons white vinegar
- 1 tablespoon Dijon mustard (or mustard of your choice)
- 1 teaspoon sugar
- Salt and pepper to taste

Instructions:

1. In a large mixing bowl, combine the shredded cabbage, grated carrots, and chopped onion. This step should take about 10 minutes.
2. In a smaller bowl, whisk together the mayonnaise, white vinegar, mustard, and sugar until smooth. This should take about 5 minutes.
3. Pour the dressing over the cabbage mixture and toss to coat evenly, ensuring all ingredients are well mixed. This step should take about 2 minutes.
4. Season with salt and pepper to taste.
5. Cover and refrigerate for at least one hour before serving to allow the flavors to meld. This chilling time is crucial for the development of flavors, so don't skip it!

Feel free to adjust the ingredients to suit your taste. Some people like to add a little celery seed, sliced bell peppers, or even a pinch of cayenne for a bit of heat. Enjoy your homemade coleslaw as a refreshing side to your favorite dishes!

Fresh Corn, Black Bean, and Feta Salad with Avocado

Prep Time:
20 minutes

Servings:
4-6

Ingredients:

- 2 ears of fresh corn, kernels removed
- 1 can (15 oz) black beans, drained and rinsed
- 2 ripe avocados, diced
- 1 cup cherry tomatoes, halved
- 1/2 cup feta cheese, crumbled
- 2 tablespoons fresh lime juice
- 2 tablespoons olive oil
- Salt and pepper to taste
- Fresh cilantro or parsley for garnish (optional)

Instructions:

1. Bring a pot of water to a boil and cook the corn kernels for 2-3 minutes until they are tender but still crisp. Then, drain and let them cool for about 5 minutes.
2. In a large salad bowl, combine the cooled corn kernels, black beans, diced avocados, and halved cherry tomatoes.
3. In a small bowl, whisk together the lime juice, olive oil, salt, and pepper to create a simple dressing. This should take about 3 minutes.
4. Drizzle the dressing over the salad and toss gently to combine, ensuring the avocado pieces don't get smashed. This step should take about 2 minutes.
5. Sprinkle the crumbled feta cheese over the top of the salad.
6. If using, garnish with chopped cilantro or parsley. This is optional and should take about 1 minute.
7. Serve immediately, or for enhanced flavor, let chill in the refrigerator for an hour before serving.

This recipe is quick and easy to prepare, ideal for a last-minute meal or when you need a dish that doesn't require much active cooking time. Enjoy your meal!

Easy Eats

Cobb Salad Recipe

Prep Time:

20 minutes

Servings:

4-6

Ingredients:

- 1 head of romaine lettuce, chopped
- 2 cooked chicken breasts, diced
- 6 slices of bacon, cooked and crumbled
- 2 ripe avocados, diced
- 4 hard-boiled eggs, peeled and sliced
- 1 cup cherry tomatoes, halved
- 1/2 cup crumbled blue cheese
- 1/2 cup red onion, thinly sliced
- 1/2 cup chopped chives or green onions
- Salt and pepper, to taste

For the Dressing:

- 1/3 cup olive oil
- 3 tablespoons red wine vinegar
- 1 teaspoon Dijon mustard
- 1 teaspoon Worcestershire sauce
- 1 small garlic clove, minced
- Salt and pepper, to taste

Instructions:

1. Prepare the Dressing:
   - In a small bowl, whisk together olive oil, red wine vinegar, Dijon mustard, Worcestershire sauce, minced garlic, salt, and pepper until well combined. Set aside.

2. Assemble the Salad:
   - In a large serving bowl, spread the chopped romaine lettuce as the base layer.
   - Arrange the diced chicken, crumbled bacon, diced avocados, sliced hard-boiled eggs, halved cherry tomatoes, crumbled blue cheese, and thinly sliced red onion in rows on top of the lettuce.

3. Add the Chives:
   - Sprinkle chopped chives or green onions over the salad for added flavor and color.

4. Dress the Salad:
   - Just before serving, drizzle the prepared dressing over the salad. Alter-natively, you can serve the dressing on the side for individuals to add to their own portions.

5. Season:
   - Season with salt and pepper to taste.

6. Serve:
   - Toss the salad gently to combine all ingredients, if desired, or serve it as is for a more traditional presentation.

Enjoy your delicious and colorful Cobb Salad, a perfect combination of flavors and textures for a satisfying and nutritious meal!

Chinese Chicken Salad Recipe

Prep Time:
20 minutes

Servings:
4-6

Ingredients:

- 2 boneless, skinless chicken breasts
- Salt and pepper, to taste
- 6 cups mixed salad greens (like romaine and iceberg lettuce)
- 1 cup shredded red cabbage
- 1 large carrot, julienned or shredded
- 1/2 cup thinly sliced red bell pepper
- 1/2 cup canned mandarin oranges, drained
- 1/4 cup sliced almonds, toasted
- 1/4 cup crispy chow mein noodles
- 2 green onions, thinly sliced
- For the Dressing:
- 1/4 cup soy sauce
- 2 tablespoons rice vinegar
- 1 tablespoon sesame oil
- 2 tablespoons vegetable oil
- 1 tablespoon honey
- 1 garlic clove, minced
- 1 teaspoon grated fresh ginger

Instructions:

1. Cook the Chicken:
- Season the chicken breasts with salt and pepper. In a skillet over medium heat, cook the chicken until it's no longer pink inside and has reached an internal temperature of 165°F (about 6-8 minutes per side). Remove from heat, let it cool, and then slice into strips.

2. Prepare the Salad Greens:
- In a large salad bowl, combine the mixed salad greens, shredded red cabbage, julienned carrot, and thinly sliced red bell pepper.

3. Make the Dressing:
- In a small bowl, whisk together soy sauce, rice vinegar, sesame oil, vegetable oil, honey, minced garlic, and grated ginger until well blended.

4. Assemble the Salad:
- Add the cooked chicken strips and mandarin oranges to the salad greens. Drizzle with the prepared dressing and toss gently to coat everything evenly.

5. Garnish:
- Sprinkle the toasted sliced almonds, crispy chow mein noodles, and sliced green onions over the top of the salad.

6. Serve:
- Serve the Chinese chicken salad immediately, offering any extra dressing on the side for those who want more.

Enjoy your vibrant and flavorful Chinese chicken salad, a perfect blend of textures and tastes, ideal for a light lunch or as a refreshing side dish!

Easy Eats

Macaroni Salad Recipe

Prep Time:
20 minutes

Servings:
4-6

Ingredients:

- 2 cups elbow macaroni
- 1/2 cup mayonnaise
- 1/4 cup sour cream
- 2 tablespoons apple cider vinegar
- 1 tablespoon Dijon mustard
- 1 teaspoon sugar
- Salt and pepper, to taste
- 1/2 cup diced celery
- 1/2 cup diced red bell pepper
- 1/4 cup finely chopped red onion
- 1/4 cup chopped fresh parsley
- 2 hard-boiled eggs, chopped (optional)

Instructions:

1. Cook the Macaroni:
- Bring a large pot of salted water to a boil. Add the elbow macaroni and cook according to the package instructions until al dente. Drain and rinse under cold water to stop the cooking process. Set aside to cool.

2. Prepare the Dressing:
- In a large mixing bowl, whisk together mayonnaise, sour cream, apple cider vinegar, Dijon mustard, sugar, salt, and pepper until well combined and smooth.

3. Add the Vegetables:
- To the dressing, add the diced celery, diced red bell pepper, finely chopped red onion, and chopped fresh parsley. Mix well to combine.

4. Combine with Macaroni:
- Add the cooled macaroni to the bowl with the dressing and vegetables. Toss gently until the macaroni is evenly coated with the dressing and the ingredients are well distributed.

5. Add Eggs (Optional):
- If using, gently fold in the chopped hard-boiled eggs.

6. Chill:
- Cover the bowl with plastic wrap and refrigerate the macaroni salad for at least 1 hour or until chilled. This allows the flavors to meld together.

7. Serve:
- Before serving, give the salad a gentle stir. Taste and adjust the seasoning with additional salt and pepper if needed.

Enjoy your creamy and flavorful macaroni salad, a classic side dish perfect for picnics, potlucks, or as a refreshing complement to any meal!

Greek Pasta Salad Recipe

Prep Time:
20 minutes

Servings:
4-6

Ingredients:

- 12 oz. rotini pasta (or any short pasta)
- 1 cup cherry tomatoes, halved
- 2 carrots, shredded
- 1/2 red onion, thinly sliced
- 1 cup Kalamata olives, pitted and halved
- 1 cup Artichoke hearts, chopped
- 1/2 cup Sundried tomatoes, chopped
- 3/4 cup feta cheese, crumbled
- 1/4 cup fresh parsley, chopped (optional)
- 1/4 cup olive oil
- 3 tbsp red wine vinegar
- 2 garlic cloves, minced
- 1 tsp dried oregano
- Salt and pepper, to taste

Instructions:

1. Cook Pasta:
- Bring a large pot of salted water to a boil. Add the pasta and cook according to package instructions until al dente. Drain and rinse under cold water to stop the cooking process. Set aside.

2. Prepare Vegetables:
- While the pasta is cooking, prepare the cherry tomatoes, cucumber, red bell pepper, and red onion. Chop and slice as directed.

3. Make the Dressing:
- In a small bowl, whisk together olive oil, red wine vinegar, minced garlic, dried oregano, salt, and pepper. Adjust seasoning to taste.

4. Combine Ingredients:
- In a large bowl, combine the cooked pasta, cherry tomatoes, carrots, red onion, and kalamata olives, chopped artichoke hearts and sundried tomatoes.

5. Add Dressing:
- Pour the dressing over the pasta salad and toss to combine, ensuring all ingredients are evenly coated.

6. Add Cheese and Herbs:
- Gently fold in the crumbled feta cheese and chopped parsley.

7. Chill (Optional):
- For best flavor, cover and refrigerate the salad for at least 30 minutes to allow the flavors to meld.

8. Serve:
- Serve the Greek pasta salad chilled or at room temperature as a refreshing side dish.

Enjoy your vibrant and flavorful Greek pasta salad, perfect for picnics, potlucks, or as a satisfying meal on its own!

Easy Eats
Breakfast and Brunch

Rise and shine to the comforting embrace of our breakfast chapter, where we pay homage to the classics and infuse a sprinkle of vibrant Mexican flair. As the first light of dawn creeps through the window, there's nothing quite like starting your day with a nourishing meal. From the simple pleasure of eggs in a basket, with their delightful meld of crispy bread and tender, runny yolks, to the colorful exuberance of a Mexican-style breakfast tostada, piled high with fresh ingredients and bold flavors, our recipes are a celebration of morning-time favorites. Whether you're setting the table for a leisurely weekend brunch or seeking a quick weekday fix before a busy day, these timeless recipes are designed to satisfy and energize. Each dish, crafted with love and care, is a wake-up call to the senses, inviting you to savor every bite and embrace the day ahead. So, let's flip the page and breakfast like champions, one delicious recipe at a time!

Your Input Matters!

Your feedback means the world to me. If you found this cookbook inspiring, practical, or simply mouthwatering, I would be immensely grateful if you could spare a moment to leave a review by scanning the code below. Your honest review not only helps fellow home cooks unlock the potential of leftovers but also provides valuable insights for future editions.

Thank you so much for your support. I wish you a lifetime of success and abundance.

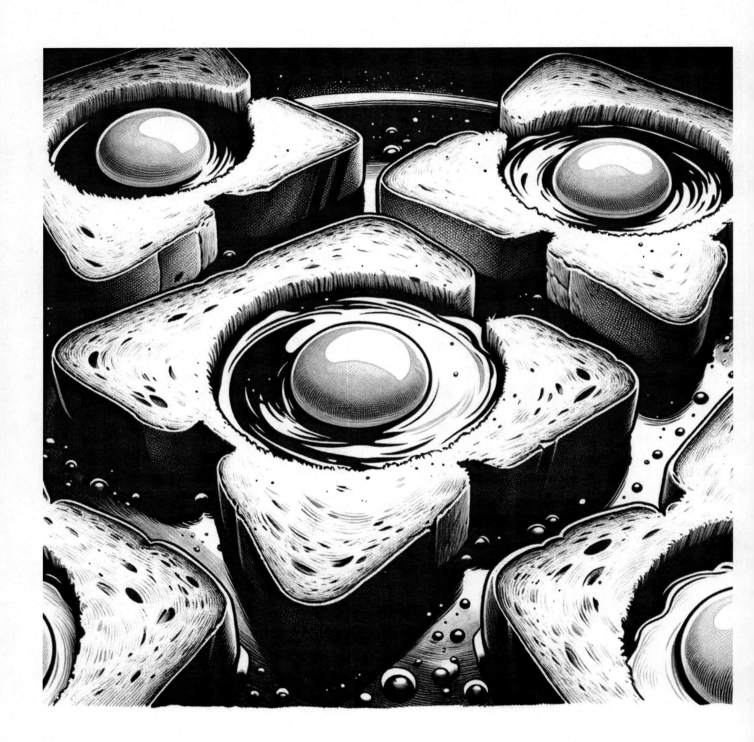

Eggs in the Basket

Prep Time:
20 minutes

Servings:
4-6

Ingredients

- 4 slices of bread
- 4 large eggs
- 2 tablespoons butter
- Salt and pepper, to taste
- Optional garnishes: chopped herbs (parsley or chives), grated cheese, a dash of paprika

Instructions:

1. Prepare the Bread:
- Using a cookie cutter or a small glass, cut a hole in the center of each slice of bread. The hole should be large enough to hold an egg.

2. Heat the Pan:
- Heat a large non-stick skillet over medium heat. Add the butter and let it melt, swirling the pan to coat the surface evenly.

3. Cook the Bread:
- Place the slices of bread, along with the cut-out circles, in the skillet. Toast for about 1 minute or until the bread is lightly golden on one side.

4. Add the Eggs:
- Flip the slices of bread over. Carefully crack an egg into the hole of each slice of bread. Season with salt and pepper.

5. Cook to Desired Doneness:
- Cook for about 2-3 minutes for a runny yolk, or longer if you prefer the yolk to be more set. If you like your egg completely cooked on top, you can cover the skillet with a lid to allow the steam to cook the top of the egg.

6. Serve:
- Using a spatula, carefully transfer each egg in the basket to a plate. Garnish with chopped herbs, grated cheese, or a dash of paprika if desired.

7. Bonus:
- Don't forget to toast the small bread circles in the pan as well! They make a great little crunchy side to your egg in the basket.

Notes:

- Eggs in the basket, also known as "egg in a hole," "toad in the hole," or "bird's nest," is a classic and fun breakfast dish.
- It's customizable; feel free to use different types of bread or add additional toppings like sliced avocado or a sprinkle of your favorite cheese.

Enjoy your delightful and simple Eggs in the Basket, a perfect start to your day!

Easy Eats

Breakfast Sandwich Recipe with Sriracha Mayo

Prep Time: 10 minutes | Cook Time: 10 minutes | Total Time: 20 minutes

Servings: 1

Ingredients

- 2 slices of your favorite bread (e.g., sourdough, whole wheat, or white bread)
- 2 tablespoons mayonnaise
- 1 teaspoon Sriracha sauce (adjust to taste)
- 1 slice of cheese (e.g., cheddar, Swiss, or American)
- 1 large egg
- 2 strips of bacon
- Butter or oil for frying
- Salt and pepper to taste Instructions

1. Cook Bacon:
- In a skillet over medium heat, cook the bacon strips until crispy. Set them aside on a paper towel to drain excess grease.

2. Prepare Sriracha Mayo:
- In a small bowl, mix together the mayonnaise and Sriracha sauce. Adjust the Sriracha amount to your preferred level of spiciness.

3. Toast Bread:
- Toast the bread slices to your desired level of crispiness.

4. Fry Egg:
- In the same skillet used for bacon (wipe out excess grease if needed), heat a bit of butter or oil over medium heat.
- Crack the egg into the skillet. Sprinkle with salt and pepper.
- Cook until the whites are set but the yolk is still runny (or to your preferred doneness).

5. Assemble Sandwich:
- Spread the Sriracha mayo on one side of each toasted bread slice.
- Place the slice of cheese on one slice of bread, followed by the fried egg.
- Add the cooked bacon strips on top of the egg.
- Close the sandwich with the other slice of bread, mayo side down.

6. Serve:
- Cut the sandwich in half if desired and serve immediately while it's warm and the cheese is melty.

Enjoy your savory and spicy breakfast sandwich, a perfect kickstart to your day! Feel free to customize the sandwich with additional ingredients like avocado, tomato, or spinach for extra flavor and nutrition.

Fried Eggs, Bacon, and Potato Breakfast with Toast

Prep Time:
20 minutes

Servings:
4-6

Ingredients:

- 4 large eggs
- 8 slices of bacon
- 2 large potatoes, peeled and diced
- 4 slices of bread (your choice)
- Salt and pepper, to taste
- Cooking oil (vegetable or canola oil)
- Optional garnishes: chopped herbs (parsley or chives), grated cheese

Instructions:

1. Prepare the Ingredients:
- Wash, peel, and dice the potatoes into small, even cubes.
- Lay out the bacon slices and bread slices.

2. Cook the Bacon:
- Heat a large skillet over medium heat.
- Lay the bacon slices in the skillet without overlapping. Cook until the bacon is golden brown and crispy, about 3-4 minutes per side.
- Once cooked, transfer the bacon to a paper towel-lined plate to drain excess grease.

3. Cook the Potatoes:
- In the same skillet with the bacon grease (you can remove some if it's too much), add the diced potatoes.
- Season with salt and pepper, and cook over medium heat, stirring occasionally, until the potatoes are golden brown and tender, about 15-20 minutes. Adjust the heat as needed to prevent burning.
- Once cooked, transfer the potatoes to a serving dish and keep warm.

4. Toast the Bread:
- While the potatoes are cooking, toast the
bread slices in a toaster to your desired level of crispiness.

5. Cook the Eggs:
- In a separate non-stick skillet, heat a small amount of cooking oil over medium heat.
- Crack the eggs into the skillet, being careful not to break the yolks. Season with salt and pepper.
- For sunny-side-up eggs, cook until the whites are set but the yolks are still runny, about 2-3 minutes. For over-easy or over-medium, flip the eggs and cook for an additional minute or two,

depending on your preference for the yolk's doneness.

6. Assemble and Serve:
   - On each plate, place two slices of toast, two eggs, a portion of the potatoes, and two slices of bacon.
   - Optional: Garnish the eggs and potatoes with chopped herbs or grated cheese.

7. Serve Immediately:
   - Serve the breakfast hot, with additional salt, pepper, or ketchup as needed.

Notes:

- This classic breakfast is hearty and satisfying, perfect for a weekend morning or brunch.
- Feel free to customize by adding sautéed vegetables to the potatoes, or using different types of bread for toast.
- Remember to adjust the cooking time for the eggs based on how well-done you prefer the yolks.

Enjoy your delicious Fried Eggs, Bacon, and Potato Breakfast with Toast, a classic start to any day!

Easy Eats

Scrambled Eggs, Bacon, Potato, and Cheese Breakfast Burrito

Prep Time:
20 minutes

Servings:
4-6

Ingredients:

- 6 large eggs
- 6 slices of bacon
- 2 large potatoes, peeled and diced
- 1 cup shredded cheddar cheese (or any preferred cheese)
- 4 large flour tortillas
- Salt and pepper, to taste
- 1 tablespoon milk (optional, for creamier eggs)
- 2 tablespoons cooking oil (vegetable or canola oil)
- Optional additions: diced onions, bell peppers, salsa, sour cream, hot sauce

Instructions:

1. Prepare the Ingredients:
- Wash, peel, and dice the potatoes into small, even cubes.
- Beat the eggs in a bowl. Add a tablespoon of milk if desired, and season with salt and pepper.

2. Cook the Bacon:
- In a large skillet, cook the bacon over medium heat until crispy, about 3-4 minutes per side. Once cooked, transfer the bacon to a paper towel-lined plate. Once cool, crumble or chop into bite-sized pieces.

3. Cook the Potatoes:
- In the same skillet with the bacon grease (remove excess grease if needed), add the diced potatoes.
- Season with salt and pepper, and cook over medium heat, stirring occasionally, until golden brown and tender, about 15-20 minutes. Adjust heat as necessary.
- Once cooked, transfer the potatoes to a bowl.

4. Scramble the Eggs:
- In a clean skillet, heat a small amount of oil over medium-low heat.
- Pour in the beaten eggs and let them sit, undisturbed, for a few seconds. Gently stir with a spatula, folding the eggs over themselves until mostly set but slightly runny.
- Remove from heat; the residual heat will finish cooking the eggs. Set aside.

5. Assemble the Burritos:
- Warm the flour tortillas in a skillet or microwave to make them more pliable.
- Lay out a tortilla, and in the center, layer scrambled eggs, cooked potatoes, crumbled bacon, and a generous sprinkle of cheese.
- Optional: Add diced onions, bell peppers, salsa, or any other desired additions.

6. Roll the Burrito:
- Fold the sides of the tortilla in over the

filling.
- Starting from the edge closest to you, roll the tortilla away from you, tucking in the sides as you go, to encase the filling completely.

7. Cook the Burrito (Optional):
- For a crispy exterior, heat a clean skillet over medium heat.
- Place the rolled burrito seam-side down and cook until golden and crispy, about 2 minutes per side.

8. Serve:
- Serve the breakfast burritos hot, with optional sides of salsa, sour cream, or hot sauce.

Notes:
- These breakfast burritos are a hearty and satisfying meal, perfect for a filling breakfast or brunch.
- They are customizable; feel free to add or substitute ingredients based on preference.
- You can wrap the burritos in foil and refrigerate or freeze for a quick and easy breakfast option on busy mornings.

Enjoy your Scrambled Eggs, Bacon, Potato, and Cheese Breakfast Burrito, a delicious and convenient way to start the day!

Easy Eats

Bacon, Cheese, and Avocado Omelette

Prep Time:
20 minutes

Servings:
4-6

Ingredients:

- 4 large eggs
- 4 slices of bacon
- 1 ripe avocado, peeled, pitted, and sliced
- 1/2 cup shredded cheese (cheddar, Swiss, or your choice)
- Salt and pepper, to taste
- tablespoons milk (optional, for fluffier omelette)
- 2 tablespoons butter or oil
- Optional garnishes: chopped chives or parsley, hot sauce, or sour cream

Instructions:

1. Prepare the Ingredients:
- Beat the eggs in a bowl. Add milk (if using), salt, and pepper. Whisk until well combined.
- Cut the avocado in half, remove the pit, and slice. Shred the cheese if it's not pre-shredded.

2. Cook the Bacon:
- In a skillet, cook the bacon over medium heat until crispy, about 3-4 minutes per side.
- Once cooked, transfer the bacon to a paper towel-lined plate. Once cool, crumble or chop into bite-sized pieces.

3. Make the Omelette:
- n a non-stick skillet, melt butter or heat oil over medium-low heat.
- Pour the beaten eggs into the skillet. Tilt the pan to ensure the eggs evenly coat the surface.
- Let the eggs cook undisturbed until they begin to set around the edges, about 2 minutes.

4. Add the Fillings:
- On one half of the omelette, sprinkle the shredded cheese, crumbled bacon, and slices of avocado.Optional: Add any additional fillings like chopped c hives, diced toma- toes, or sautéed onions if desired.

5. Fold the Omelette:
- Once the eggs are mostly set but still slightly runny on top, carefully fold the omelette in half with a spatula, covering the fillings.
- Let cook for another minute or so until the cheese is melted and the eggs are fully set.

6. Serve:
- Carefully slide the omelette onto a plate.
- Optional: Garnish with additional chopped chives, parsley, a dash of hot sauce, or a dollop of sour cream.

7. Enjoy:
- Serve the bacon, cheese, and avocado omelette hot for a delicious and satisfying meal.

Notes:

- This omelette is a rich and satisfying dish, perfect for a hearty breakfast or brunch.
- The combination of creamy avocado, crispy bacon, and melted cheese is both flavorful and filling.
- Feel free to adjust the fillings according to your preference or dietary needs.

Enjoy your Bacon, Cheese, and Avocado Omelette, a delightful blend of flavors to kickstart your day!

Easy Eats

Denver Omelette

Prep Time:
20 minutes

Servings:
4-6

Ingredients:

- 4 large eggs
- 1/2 cup diced ham
- 1/4 cup diced green bell pepper
- 1/4 cup diced onion
- 1/2 cup shredded cheddar cheese (or your preferred cheese)
- Salt and pepper, to taste
- 2 tablespoons milk (optional, for fluffier omelette)
- 2 tablespoons butter or oil
- Optional garnishes: chopped parsley, hot sauce, or sour cream

Instructions:

1. Prepare the Ingredients:
- Beat the eggs in a bowl. Add milk (if using), salt, and pepper. Whisk until well combined.
- Dice the ham, green bell pepper, and onion into small, even pieces.

2. Cook the Vegetables and Ham:
- In a non-stick skillet, heat 1 tablespoon of butter or oil over medium heat.
- Add the diced onion and green bell pepper. Sauté until they begin to soften, about 3-4 minutes.
- Add the diced ham and cook for another 2-3 minutes, until the ham is lightly browned. Remove the mixture from the skillet and set aside.

3. Make the Omelette:
- In the same skillet, add the remaining butter or oil and heat over medium-low heat.
- Pour the beaten eggs into the skillet. Tilt the pan to ensure the eggs evenly coat the surface.
- Let the eggs cook undisturbed until they begin to set around the edges, about 2 minutes.

4. Add the Fillings:
- On one half of the omelette, sprinkle the shredded cheese and evenly distribute the sautéed ham, onion, and bell pepper mixture.
- Optional: Add any additional fillings or seasonings if desired.

5. Fold the Omelette:
- Once the eggs are mostly set but still slightly runny on top, carefully fold the omelette in half with a spatula, covering the fillings.

- Let cook for another minute or so until the cheese is melted and the eggs are fully set.

6. Serve:
- Carefully slide the omelette onto a plate.
- Optional: Garnish with chopped parsley, a dash of hot sauce, or a dollop of sour cream.

7. Enjoy:
- Serve the Denver Omelette hot for a classic and hearty meal.

Notes:

- The Denver Omelette, also known as a Western Omelette, is a filling and flavorful dish, perfect for a satisfying breakfast or brunch.
- he combination of ham, bell pepper, onion, and cheese is classic, but feel free to adjust the fillings according to your taste or what you have on hand.
- this omelette pairs well with toast, hash browns, or a side of fruit for a complete meal.

Enjoy your Denver Omelette, a classic American breakfast favorite!

Spanish Omelette with Chorizo and Cheese

Prep Time:
20 minutes

Servings:
4-6

Ingredients:

- 4 large eggs
- 2 large potatoes, peeled and thinly sliced
- 1 medium onion, thinly sliced
- 1/2 cup diced chorizo
- 1/2 cup shredded cheese (Manchego, cheddar, or your preferred cheese)
- 3/4 cup olive oil (for frying)
- Salt and pepper, to taste
- 1 ripe avocado, sliced
- Sour cream, for topping
- Optional: chopped parsley or chives for garnish

Instructions:

1. Prepare the Ingredients:
- Peel and thinly slice the potatoes and onion. Dice the chorizo into small pieces. Beat the eggs in a bowl and season with salt and pepper.

2. Cook the Potatoes, Onion, and Chorizo:
- Heat the olive oil in a large, non-stick frying pan over medium heat.
- Add the sliced potatoes and onion to the pan. Cook, stirring occasionally, until the potatoes are tender but not browned, about 15-20 minutes.
- Add the diced chorizo to the pan during the last 5 minutes of cooking.
- Once cooked, use a slotted spoon to transfer the potatoes, onion, and chorizo to a bowl. Reserve the oil.

3. Combine Eggs with Potato Mixture:
- Pour the beaten eggs over the cooked potatoes, onions, and chorizo, gently mixing to ensure an even distribution. Let the mixture sit for a few minutes.

4. Cook the Omelette:
- In the same frying pan, remove excess oil (leave just enough to coat the pan) and heat over medium heat.
- Pour the egg, potato, chorizo, and onion mixture into the pan, spreading it evenly.
- Sprinkle the shredded cheese on top of the mixture.
- Cook for about 5 minutes, until the bottom is lightly golden and the top begins to set.

5. Flip the Omelette:
- Place a large plate over the frying pan. Carefully flip the pan so that the omelette transfers onto the plate.

- Slide the omelette back into the pan, uncooked side down, and cook for another 3-5 minutes until fully set.

6. Serve:

- Slide the omelette onto a plate. Top with slices of avocado and a generous dollop of sour cream.
- Optional: Garnish with chopped parsley or chives.

7. Enjoy:

- This Spanish Omelette variation is a hearty and flavorful dish, perfect for any meal.

Notes:

- The addition of chorizo and cheese brings a delicious depth of flavor to the traditional Spanish Omelette.
- The creamy avocado and sour cream add freshness and richness to the dish, balancing the flavors.
- This omelette can be served hot or at room temperature and is great for breakfast, brunch, or even as a light dinner.

Enjoy your Spanish Omelette with Chorizo and Cheese, a delightful twist on a classic Spanish dish!

Easy Eats

Steak and Eggs Skillet (see Dinners)

Prep Time:
20 minutes

Servings:
4-6

Ingredients:

- Leftover steak, chopped into bite-sized pieces
- 4 large eggs
- 1 small onion, diced
- 1 bell pepper, diced
- 2 medium potatoes, diced
- 1/2 cup shredded cheese (cheddar or Monterey Jack)
- Salt and pepper, to taste
- 2 tbsp olive oil
- Fresh parsley or chives, chopped for garnish
- Hot sauce (optional)

Instructions:

1. Heat olive oil in a large skillet over medium heat.
2. Add the diced potatoes to the skillet and season with salt and pepper. Cook until they are golden and tender, stirring occasionally.
3. Add the diced onion and bell pepper to the skillet. Cook until the vegetables are softened.
4. Stir in the chopped leftover steak and cook for another 2-3 minutes, just to heat the steak through.
5. Make four wells in the mixture and crack an egg into each well.
6. Cover the skillet with a lid and cook until the egg whites are set but the yolks are still runny, or to your desired level of doneness.
7. Sprinkle shredded cheese over the top and cover for another minute to let the cheese melt.
8. Garnish with chopped parsley or chives, and serve hot with a dash of hot sauce if desired.

Enjoy a hearty and delicious breakfast skillet that makes the most of your leftover steak!

Chilaquiles with Corn Tortilla Chips, Beans, Cheese, and Fried Eggs

Prep Time:
20 minutes

Servings:
4-6

Ingredients:

- 4 cups corn tortilla chips
- 1 can (15 oz) black beans or refried beans
- 1 cup red enchilada sauce (or green sauce as a substitute)
- 4 large eggs
- 1 cup shredded cheese (cheddar, Monterey Jack, or Mexican blend)
- 2 tablespoons vegetable oil or olive oil
- Optional garnishes: chopped cilantro, sliced avocado, diced red onion, sour cream, crumbled queso fresco

Instructions:

1. Preheat the Oven:
- Preheat your oven to 375°F (190°C).

2. Warm the Beans:
- If using canned black beans, drain and rinse them. Warm the beans in a small pot over low heat. If using refried beans, simply warm them in a pot or in the microwave.

3. Prepare the Baking Dish:
- Lightly grease a baking dish with some oil.

4. 1. Layer the Chilaquiles:
- Spread half of the tortilla chips in the bottom of the baking dish.
- Spoon half of the warmed beans over the chips.
- Drizzle half of the red enchilada sauce (or green sauce, if preferred) over the beans.
- Sprinkle half of the shredded cheese over the sauce.
- Repeat with another layer of tortilla chips, beans, sauce, and cheese.

5. Bake:
- Place the baking dish in the preheated oven and bake for about 15 minutes, or until the cheese is melted and bubbly.

6. Fry the Eggs:
- While the chilaquiles are baking, heat the oil in a frying pan over medium heat.
- Crack the eggs into the pan and fry them to your preferred doneness. Season with a little salt and pepper.

7. Assemble and Serve:
- Remove the baked chilaquiles from the oven.
- Carefully place the fried eggs on top of the baked chilaquiles.
- Optional: Garnish with chopped cilantro, sliced avocado, diced red onion, a dollop of sour cream, and/or crumbled queso fresco.
- Serve hot and enjoy!

Notes:

- Chilaquiles is a traditional Mexican breakfast dish that's a great way to use up leftover tortilla chips.
- You can easily customize this dish by using green enchilada sauce instead of red for a different flavor profile.
- Feel free to adjust the amount of cheese and toppings according to your preference.

Enjoy your Chilaquiles with Corn Tortilla Chips, Beans, Cheese, and Fried Eggs, a delicious start to your day!

Easy Eats

Breakfast Tostada Recipe

Prep Time: 10 minutes Cook Time: 10 minutes Total Time: 20 minutes

Servings: 2

Ingredients

- 2 tostada shells
- 1 cup refried beans
- 1 cup shredded cheese (cheddar or Mexican blend)
- 2 large eggs
- 1 ripe avocado, sliced
- 1/2 cup avocado salsa (store-bought or homemade)
- Salt and pepper, to taste
- Olive oil or cooking spray
- Optional toppings: chopped cilantro, sliced jalapeños, sour cream

Instructions

1. Preheat Oven: Preheat your oven to 375°F (190°C).

2. Prepare Tostadas:
   - Spread a generous layer of refried beans over each tostada shell.
   - Sprinkle shredded cheese on top of the beans, covering them evenly.

3. Heat Tostadas:
   - Place the prepared tostadas on a baking sheet.
   - Bake in the preheated oven for about 5-7 minutes, or until the cheese is melted and bubbly.

4. Fry Eggs:
   - While the tostadas are in the oven, heat a non-stick skillet over medium heat.
   - Add a little olive oil or cooking spray to the pan.
   - Crack the eggs into the skillet, and fry them to your desired level of doneness. Season with salt and pepper.

5. Assemble Tostadas:
   - Remove the tostadas from the oven.
   - Carefully place a fried egg on top of each tostada.
   - Add sliced avocado over the eggs.
   - Generously spoon avocado salsa over the top.

6. Garnish and Serve:
   - If desired, garnish with chopped cilantro, sliced jalapeños, or a dollop of sour cream.
   - Serve immediately while warm and enjoy your delicious breakfast tostada!

Feel free to customize this recipe with additional toppings or by using different types of cheese or salsa. It's a versatile dish that's perfect for a hearty breakfast or brunch!

Easy Eats

Spinach and Parmesan Quiche Recipe

Prep Time:
20 minutes

Servings:
4-6

Ingredients:

- 1 pie crust (store-bought or homemade)
- 1 tablespoon olive oil
- 1 small onion, finely chopped
- 2 cups fresh spinach, roughly chopped
- 4 large eggs
- 1 cup heavy cream
- 1 cup grated Parmesan cheese
- 1/2 teaspoon salt
- 1/4 teaspoon black pepper
- Optional: 4 strips of bacon, cooked and crumbled

Instructions:

1. Preheat your oven to 375°F (190°C). If using a store-bought pie crust, allow it to thaw as per package instructions.
2. In a skillet, heat olive oil over medium heat. Add chopped onion and sauté until translucent, about 3-4 minutes.
3. Add the chopped spinach to the skillet and cook until wilted, about 2-3 minutes. If using bacon, add the cooked and crumbled bacon to the spinach mixture. Remove from heat and set aside.
4. In a mixing bowl, whisk together the eggs, heavy cream, grated Parmesan cheese, salt, and pepper until well combined.
5. If using a homemade pie crust, roll out the dough and fit it into a 9-inch pie dish. Trim and crimp the edges as desired. If using a store-bought crust, place it in the pie dish.
6. Spread the spinach (and bacon) mixture evenly over the bottom of the pie crust.
7. Pour the egg and cheese mixture over the spinach layer, ensuring the ingredients are evenly distributed.
8. Place the quiche in the preheated oven and bake for 35-40 minutes, or until the quiche is set in the center and the crust is golden brown.
9. Remove from the oven and let it cool for a few minutes before slicing.
10. Serve warm and enjoy your savory Spinach and Parmesan Quiche. It's perfect for breakfast, brunch, or even dinner!

Traditional Pancakes

Prep Time:
20 minutes

Servings:
4-6

Ingredients:

- 1 1/2 cups all-purpose flour
- 3 1/2 tsp baking powder
- 1 tsp salt
- 1 tbsp granulated sugar
- 1 1/4 cups milk (you can use whole milk for a richer flavor)
- 1 large egg
- 3 tbsp melted butter
- Additional butter or oil for the pan
- Maple syrup, for serving
- Optional toppings: fresh berries, whipped cream, chocolate chips, or sliced bananas

Instructions:

1. Dry Ingredients: In a large mixing bowl, sift together the flour, baking powder, salt, and sugar.
2. Wet Ingredients: In a separate bowl, whisk together the milk, egg, and melted butter.
3. Combine: Pour the wet ingredients into the dry ingredients and stir just until combined. Be careful not to overmix; it's okay if there are a few lumps.
4. Heat the Pan: Preheat a non-stick skillet or frying pan over medium heat. Add a small amount of butter or oil to lightly coat the pan.
5. Cook the Pancakes: Pour 1/4 cup portions of the batter onto the skillet. Cook until bubbles form on the surface of the pancake and the edges look set (about 2-3 minutes). Flip the pancake and cook for another 1-2 minutes on the other side, or until golden brown and cooked through.
6. Serve: Remove the pancakes from the skillet and repeat with the remaining batter. Serve the pancakes warm with a generous drizzle of maple syrup and your choice of toppings.

Tips:

- For fluffier pancakes, let the batter sit for 5-10 minutes before cooking. This allows the baking powder to activate, giving the pancakes a lighter texture.
- Adjust the heat as needed. If the pancakes are browning too quickly, reduce the heat. If they're taking too long to cook, increase the heat slightly.
- You can add a twist to your traditional pancakes by adding blueberries, chocolate chips, or nuts to the batter before cooking.

Enjoy your classic and fluffy pancakes!

Easy Eats

Banana Nut Oat Pancakes

Prep Time:
20 minutes

Servings:
4-6

Ingredients:

- 1 ripe banana
- 2 large eggs
- 1/2 cup rolled oats
- 1/4 cup chopped walnuts or pecans
- 1/2 tsp baking powder
- 1/2 tsp vanilla extract
- 1/4 tsp cinnamon (optional)
- Pinch of salt
- Maple syrup or honey, for serving
- Fresh fruits (like strawberries, blueberries) for topping
- Butter or oil for cooking

Instructions:

1. Blend the Base: In a blender, combine the ripe banana, eggs, rolled oats, baking powder, vanilla extract, cinnamon, and a pinch of salt. Blend until the mixture is smooth and well-combined.
2. Add Nuts: Stir in the chopped walnuts or pecans using a spoon.
3. Preheat the Pan: Heat a non-stick skillet or frying pan over medium heat. Add a small amount of butter or oil to lightly coat the pan.
4. Cook the Pancakes: Pour 1/4 cup portions of the batter onto the skillet. Cook until bubbles form on the surface of the pancake and the edges appear set (about 2-3 minutes). Flip the pancake and cook for an additional 1-2 minutes on the other side, or until golden brown and cooked through.
5. Serve: Remove the pancakes from the skillet and repeat with the remaining batter. Serve the pancakes warm with a drizzle of maple syrup or honey and top with fresh fruits of your choice.

Tips:

- For a protein-packed version, you can add a scoop of your favorite protein powder to the batter.
- If you're feeling adventurous, you can add chocolate chips, coconut flakes, or even a spoonful of peanut butter or almond butter to the batter.
- These pancakes can be stored in the refrigerator for up to 2 days and reheated in the microwave or toaster.

Enjoy your delicious and healthy breakfast!

Easy Eats

Blueberry Pancake Recipe

Prep Time: 15 minutes Cook Time: 10 minutes Total Time: 25 minutes

Servings: 4

Ingredients

- 1 1/2 cups all-purpose flour
- 2 tablespoons sugar
- 1 tablespoon baking powder
- 1/2 teaspoon salt
- 1 1/4 cups milk
- 1 large egg
- 3 tablespoons unsalted butter, melted (plus more for greasing the pan)
- 1 teaspoon vanilla extract
- 1 cup fresh blueberries (or frozen if out of season)
- Optional: powdered sugar or maple syrup for serving

Instructions

1. Dry Ingredients:
- In a large mixing bowl, whisk together flour, sugar, baking powder, and salt.

2. Wet Ingredients:
- In another bowl, beat the egg and then mix in the milk, melted butter, and vanilla extract.

3. Combine:
- Pour the wet ingredients into the dry ingredients.
- Gently stir together until just combined. Be careful not to overmix; a few lumps are okay.

4. Add Blueberries:
- Gently fold in the blueberries. If using frozen blueberries, do not thaw them before adding.

5. Cook Pancakes:
- Heat a non-stick skillet or griddle over medium heat and lightly grease it with butter.
- For each pancake, pour about 1/4 cup of batter onto the skillet.
- Cook until bubbles form on the surface and the edges look set, about 2-3 minutes.
- Flip the pancake and cook for another 1-2 minutes until golden brown and cooked through.

6. Serve:
- Serve the blueberry pancakes warm.
- Optional: Dust with powdered sugar or drizzle with maple syrup.

Enjoy your fluffy and delicious blueberry pancakes, perfect for a weekend breakfast or a special brunch! Feel free to adjust the amount of blueberries to your preference or add other toppings like whipped cream or sliced bananas.

Classic French Toast Breakfast

Prep Time:
20 minutes

Servings:
4-6

Ingredients:

- 4 thick slices of bread (preferably day-old, such as brioche, challah, or French bread)
- 2 large eggs
- 1 cup whole milk or half-and-half
- 2 tablespoons granulated sugar
- 1 teaspoon pure vanilla extract
- 1/2 teaspoon ground cinnamon
- A pinch of nutmeg (optional)
- A pinch of salt
- Butter or oil, for frying
- Toppings:
- Maple syrup or honey
- Fresh berries (blueberries, strawberries, raspberries)
- Powdered sugar (for dusting)
- Whipped cream (optional)
- Sliced bananas or other fruits (optional)

Instructions:

1. Prepare the Custard Mixture:
- In a mixing bowl, beat the eggs, then add the milk or half-and-half, granulated sugar, vanilla extract, cinnamon, nutmeg (if using), and salt. Whisk until all ingredients are combined well.

2. Soak the Bread:
- Dip each slice of bread into the egg mixture, ensuring both sides are well-coated. Allow each slice to soak for about 20-30 seconds on each side so that the bread absorbs the mixture but doesn't become too soggy.

3. Cook the French Toast:
- Heat a large skillet or non-stick frying pan over medium heat. Add a generous pat of butter or a splash of oil.
- Once the butter is melted and sizzling (or the oil is hot), place the soaked bread slices into the pan. Cook for about 2-4 minutes on each side, or until golden brown and crispy.

4. Serve:
- Transfer the cooked French toast to plates. Dust with powdered sugar and top with fresh berries, sliced bananas, or your choice of fruits.
- Drizzle with maple syrup or honey, and if you're feeling indulgent, add a dollop of whipped cream.
- Serve hot and enjoy!

Notes:
- Day-old bread works best for French toast as it absorbs the custard mixture without becoming overly soggy.
- Feel free to adjust the sugar, cinnamon, and vanilla to your preference.
- French toast can also be topped with nuts, chocolate chips, or even a sprinkle of cocoa powder for variation.
- This dish pairs well with a side of crispy bacon or sausage for a full breakfast experience.

Enjoy your Classic French Toast Breakfast, a timeless dish that's sure to delight your taste buds!

Dinner and Leftovers

Step into the inviting realm of our "Dinner and Leftovers" chapter, where each thoughtfully curated dinner menu is not only an end-of-day feast but also the beginning of tomorrow's culinary adventure. We understand that a satisfying dinner is the cornerstone of family gatherings and solo indulgences alike, and the magic need not end with the evening's last bite. With every sumptuous spread presented in these pages, we offer a clever twist on repurposing your leftovers, transforming them into innovative breakfasts, energizing lunches, or entirely new dinner delights.

Imagine savoring a robust lasagna only to rediscover its flavors in a hearty soup the next day, or the evening's grilled salmon reborn as a refreshing salad topper when the noon bell tolls. Here, we embrace the sustainability and creativity of cooking, ensuring that no morsel of your culinary masterpiece goes to waste. Let's turn the day's end into tomorrow's beginning with meals that keep on giving.

Herb Roasted Chicken and Vegetables

Prep Time:
20 minutes

Servings:
4-6

Ingredients:

- 4 boneless, skinless chicken breasts
- 2 carrots, peeled and sliced
- 2 potatoes, peeled and cubed
- 1 red bell pepper, sliced
- 1 zucchini, sliced
- 3 tablespoons olive oil
- 2 teaspoons dried mixed herbs (such as thyme, rosemary, oregano)
- Salt and pepper, to taste
- 1 teaspoon garlic powder

Instructions:

1. Preheat your oven to 400°F (200°C).
2. In a large bowl, toss the carrots, potatoes, red bell pepper, and zucchini with 2 tablespoons of olive oil, 1 teaspoon of mixed herbs, salt, and pepper.
3. Spread the vegetables in a single layer on a baking sheet.
4. In the same bowl, add the chicken breasts. Toss them with the remaining olive oil, mixed herbs, garlic powder, salt, and pepper.
5. Place the seasoned chicken breasts on top of the vegetables.
6. Roast in the oven for about 25-30 minutes, or until the chicken is cooked through and the vegetables are tender.
7. Serve warm.

Easy Eats

Chicken and Veggie Quesadillas Using Leftovers

Prep Time:
20 minutes

Servings:
4-6

Ingredients:

- Leftover roasted chicken and vegetables from Recipe 1
- 4 large flour tortillas
- 1 cup shredded cheese (Cheddar or Monterey Jack)
- 2 tablespoons olive oil or butter
- Sour cream and salsa, for serving (optional)

Instructions:

1. Shred the leftover roasted chicken into small pieces. Chop the roasted vegetables into bite-sized pieces if necessary.
2. Lay out the flour tortillas on a flat surface. On one half of each tortilla, evenly distribute the shredded chicken, chopped vegetables, and shredded cheese.
3. Fold the other half of the tortilla over the filling to create a half-moon shape.
4. Heat a large skillet over medium heat. Add a little olive oil or butter.
5. Place one quesadilla in the skillet and cook until the bottom is golden brown, about 2-3 minutes. Carefully flip and cook the other side until golden and the cheese is melted.
6. Repeat with the remaining quesadillas.
7. Cut each quesadilla into wedges and serve with sour cream and salsa if desired.

These two recipes offer a perfect combination for a weekday dinner and a creative use of leftovers. The roasted chicken and vegetables provide a wholesome meal, while the leftover ingredients transform into a delicious and easy quesadilla dish for the following day.

Chicken Parmesan with Fettuccine Pasta and Caesar Salad

Prep Time:
20 minutes

Servings:
4-6

Ingredients:

For Chicken Parmesan:

- 4 boneless, skinless chicken breasts
- Salt and pepper, to taste
- 1 cup all-purpose flour
- 2 large eggs, beaten
- 2 cups breadcrumbs, preferably Italian seasoned
- 1 cup grated Parmesan cheese
- Olive oil, for frying
- 2 cups marinara sauce
- 2 cups shredded mozzarella cheese
- Fresh basil leaves, for garnish

For Fettuccine Pasta:

- 12 ounces fettuccine pasta
- Salt, for pasta water
- 2 tablespoons olive oil
- 2 cloves garlic, minced
- 1 cup heavy cream
- 1 cup grated Parmesan cheese
- Fresh parsley, chopped, for garnish

For Caesar Salad:

- 1 head romaine lettuce, chopped
- 1 cup croutons
- 1/2 cup grated Parmesan cheese
- Caesar dressing (store-bought or homemade)

Instructions:

1. Prepare the Chicken Parmesan:

- Preheat the oven to 400°F (200°C).
- Season chicken breasts with salt and pepper. Dredge in flour, dip in beaten eggs, and coat with breadcrumbs mixed with grated Parmesan cheese.
- Heat olive oil in a large skillet over medium heat. Fry the chicken until golden brown on both sides. Transfer to a baking dish.
- Spoon marinara sauce over each chicken breast, and top with shredded mozzarella cheese.
- Bake for 20-25 minutes, or until the cheese is bubbly and golden. Garnish with fresh basil leaves.

2. Cook the Fettuccine:

- Cook fettuccine pasta in salted boiling water according to package instructions. Drain and set aside.

- In the same pot, heat olive oil and sauté garlic until fragrant. Add heavy cream and bring to a simmer.
- Stir in grated Parmesan cheese until melted and the sauce thickens. Toss the cooked pasta in the sauce. Garnish with chopped parsley.

3. Assemble the Caesar Salad:

- In a large bowl, combine chopped romaine lettuce, croutons, and grated Parmesan cheese.
- Toss with Caesar dressing until evenly coated.

Serve the chicken Parmesan with a side of creamy fettuccine pasta and a fresh Caesar salad. Enjoy your delicious Italian-inspired meal!

Easy Eats

Chicken Parmesan Sandwich with Fettuccine Soup Using Leftovers

Prep Time:
20 minutes

Servings:
4-6

Additional Ingredients:

- 2-4 hoagie rolls or ciabatta bread
- Butter, for toasting bread
- 2 cups chicken or vegetable broth
- 1 cup milk or cream
- 1 tablespoon flour (optional, for thickening)

Instructions:

1. Chicken Parmesan Sandwich:

- Slice the leftover chicken Parmesan into pieces that fit the bread.
- Lightly butter the hoagie rolls or ciabatta and toast them until golden.
- Place the chicken Parmesan pieces on the toasted bread, adding extra marinara sauce and cheese if desired.
- Warm in the oven or a toaster oven until the cheese is melted and bubbly.

2. Fettuccine Alfredo Soup:

- In a pot, bring the chicken or vegetable broth to a simmer.
- Cut the leftover fettuccine pasta into smaller pieces and add to the broth.
- Stir in milk or cream and bring to a light simmer. If you prefer a thicker soup, mix 1 tablespoon of flour with a little water to make a paste, then stir into the soup to thicken.
- Season with salt and pepper to taste. Simmer for a few minutes until the pasta is heated through.

Serve the Chicken Parmesan sandwich with a side of warm Fettuccine Alfredo soup. This meal repurposes your leftovers into a whole new delicious experience!

Chicken Piccata Recipe with Asparagus and Rice Pilaf

Prep Time:
20 minutes

Servings:
4-6

Ingredients:

- 4 boneless, skinless chicken breasts
- Salt and pepper to taste
- 1/2 cup all-purpose flour
- 4 tablespoons olive oil
- 1/4 cup fresh lemon juice
- 1/2 cup chicken broth
- 1/4 cup capers
- 2 tablespoons butter
- Chopped parsley for garnish
- 1 bunch of asparagus, trimmed
- 1 box of store-bought rice pilaf

Instructions:

1. Prepare Chicken: Season chicken breasts with salt and pepper. Dredge them in flour, shaking off any excess.
2. Cook Chicken: In a large skillet, heat 2 tablespoons of olive oil over medium--high heat. Add chicken and cook for about 4-5 minutes on each side, until golden and cooked through. Remove chicken and set aside.
3. Make Sauce: In the same skillet, add lemon juice, chicken broth, and capers. Bring to a boil, scraping up any browned bits from the pan. Reduce heat and simmer for 5 minutes.
4. Finish Sauce: Stir in butter until melted and incorporated. Return chicken to the pan and coat with the sauce. Garnish with chopped parsley.
5. Cook Asparagus: In another pan, heat the remaining 2 tablespoons of olive oil. Add asparagus and cook until tender but still crisp, about 4-5 minutes. Season with salt and pepper.
6. Prepare Rice Pilaf: Cook the rice pilaf according to the package instructions.
7. Serve: Plate the chicken piccata with a generous spoonful of sauce, a side of asparagus, and rice pilaf.

Chicken Piccata Sandwich Using Leftovers

Prep Time:
20 minutes

Servings:
4-6

Ingredients:

- Slices of your favorite bread
- Leftover chicken piccata, sliced
- Mayonnaise or aioli
- Lettuce leaves
- Tomato slices
- Cheese slices (optional)

Instructions:

1. Prepare Bread: Lightly toast the bread slices.
2. Assemble Sandwich: Spread mayonnaise or aioli on one side of each bread slice. On one slice, layer lettuce, tomato, slices of leftover chicken piccata, and cheese if using.
3. Complete Sandwich: Top with the other slice of bread, mayonnaise side down.
4. Serve: Cut the sandwich in half and serve immediately, perhaps with a side of chips or a salad.

Easy Eats

Spatchcock Chicken with Potatoes and Brussels Sprouts Recipe

Prep Time:
20 minutes

Servings:
4-6

Ingredients:

- 1 whole chicken (about 4-5 pounds)
- 2 pounds small potatoes, halved
- 1 pound Brussels sprouts, trimmed and halved
- 4 tablespoons olive oil
- 2 cloves garlic, minced
- 2 teaspoons smoked paprika
- 1 teaspoon dried thyme
- Salt and pepper, to taste
- Fresh parsley, chopped (for garnish)

Instructions:

1. Preheat your oven to 425°F (220°C).
2. To spatchcock the chicken, place it breast-side down. Using kitchen shears, cut along both sides of the backbone and remove it. Flip the chicken over and press down on the breastbone to flatten it.
3. In a small bowl, mix 2 tablespoons olive oil, minced garlic, smoked paprika, dried thyme, salt, and pepper.
4. Rub the chicken all over with the spice mixture, ensuring to get under the skin as well.
5. Toss the potatoes and Brussels sprouts with the remaining 2 tablespoons of olive oil, salt, and pepper.
6. Place the chicken in the center of a large roasting pan. Arrange the potatoes and Brussels sprouts around the chicken.
7. Roast in the preheated oven for about 45-55 minutes or until the chicken is cooked through and the vegetables are tender.
8. Garnish with fresh parsley before serving.

Easy Eats

Chicken Enchiladas Using Leftovers

Prep Time:
20 minutes

Servings:
4-6

Ingredients:

- Leftover spatchcock chicken, shredded
- 10-12 corn tortillas
- 2 cups enchilada sauce
- 2 cups shredded cheese (Mexican blend or cheddar)
- 1 small onion, diced
- 1 bell pepper, diced
- 2 cloves garlic, minced
- 1 teaspoon cumin
- Salt and pepper, to taste
- Fresh cilantro, chopped (for garnish)
- Sour cream (for serving)

Instructions:

1. Preheat your oven to 350°F (175°C).
2. In a pan, sauté onion, bell pepper, and garlic until softened. Add the shredded chicken, cumin, salt, and pepper. Cook for a few minutes until well combined.
3. Pour a thin layer of enchilada sauce in the bottom of a baking dish.
4. Warm the tortillas slightly to make them pliable. Fill each tortilla with the chicken mixture and a sprinkle of cheese. Roll up and place seam- side down in the baking dish.
5. Pour the remaining enchilada sauce over the rolled tortillas and sprinkle with the remaining cheese.
6. Bake for about 20-25 minutes or until the cheese is melted and bubbly.
7. Garnish with fresh cilantro and serve with sour cream.

Now, let's create a black and white sketch of one of these recipes.

Stuffed Chicken Breast with Mozzarella, Pesto, and Sun-Dried Tomatoes

Prep Time:
20 minutes

Servings:
4-6

Ingredients:

- 4 boneless, skinless chicken breasts
- 1 cup mozzarella cheese, shredded
- 1/2 cup pesto
- 1/2 cup sun-dried tomatoes, chopped
- Salt and pepper to taste
- 2 tablespoons olive oil

Instructions:

1. Preheat Oven: Preheat your oven to 375°F (190°C).
2. Prepare Chicken: Make a pocket in each chicken breast by cutting a slit along the side. Be careful not to cut all the way through.
3. Stuff Chicken: Season the inside of each chicken breast with salt and pepper. Spread about 2 tablespoons of pesto inside each pocket. Then stuff with mozzarella cheese and sun-dried tomatoes.
4. Seal Chicken: Close the pocket and secure with toothpicks if needed.
5. Cook Chicken: Heat olive oil in a large oven-safe skillet over medium-high heat. Sear the chicken breasts for about 3 minutes on each side, until golden brown.
6. Bake: Transfer the skillet to the preheated oven and bake for 20-25 minutes, or until the chicken is cooked through.
7. Serve: Let the chicken rest for a few minutes before serving. Remove toothpicks before eating.

Leftover Stuffed Chicken Panini Using Leftovers

Prep Time:
20 minutes

Servings:
4-6

Ingredients:

- Leftover stuffed chicken breast, sliced
- 4 slices of sourdough bread
- 2 tablespoons butter
- 4 slices of provolone cheese
- Additional pesto for spreading

Instructions:

1. Preheat Panini Press: If you don't have a panini press, you can use a skillet.
2. Prepare Sandwich: Butter one side of each slice of sourdough bread. On the unbuttered side, spread a thin layer of pesto.
3. Assemble Panini: Place a slice of provolone cheese on the pesto side of two bread slices. Add sliced leftover stuffed chicken on top of the cheese. Top with another slice of provolone cheese and the remaining bread slices, buttered side facing out.
4. Cook Panini: Place the sandwiches in the panini press or skillet. Cook until the bread is golden and crispy, and the cheese has melted.
5. Serve: Slice the panini in half and serve warm.

Sticky Asian Chicken Legs with Asian Cabbage Salad and Fried Rice

Prep Time:
20 minutes

Servings:
4-6

1. For the Chicken Legs:
- Marinate chicken legs using the Sweet and Spicy Asian Marinade from Sauces and Dips Chapter. In a large ziplock bag put the legs in with the marinade and make sure all the legs are covered.
- Chill in the fridge for at least an hour, but overnight is better.

2. For the Oven:
- Preheat oven to 375°F (190°C).
- Place marinated chicken legs on a baking sheet lined with parchment paper.
- Bake for 35-40 minutes or until fully cooked and the skin is crispy.

3. For the Air Fryer:
- Preheat air fryer to 380°F (190°C).
- Place chicken legs in the air fryer basket, ensuring they are not overcrowded.
- Cook for 20-25 minutes, flipping halfway through, until fully cooked and crispy.

4. Asian Cabbage Salad:
- 4 cups shredded cabbage
- 1 cup shredded carrots
- 1/2 cup slivered almonds
- 2 green onions, chopped
- Toss with Japanese Mayo Salad Dressing from Sauces and Dips chapter

5. Asian Fried Rice:
- 4 cups cooked rice (preferably day-old)
- 2 tablespoons sesame oil
- 2 eggs, beaten
- 1 cup mixed vegetables (peas, carrots, corn)
- 2 tablespoons soy sauce

1. Heat sesame oil in a large skillet over medium heat.
2. Add beaten eggs and scramble until cooked. Remove and set aside.
3. In the same skillet, add mixed vegetables and stir-fry for a few minutes.
4. Add rice and soy sauce, mixing well.
5. Add scrambled eggs back in and mix until well combined.

Easy Eats

Asian Chicken Lettuce Wraps Using Leftovers

Prep Time:
20 minutes

Servings:
4-6

Ingredients:

- Leftover sticky Asian chicken legs, shredded
- Lettuce leaves (butter lettuce works well)
- Shredded carrots
- Chopped green onions
- Hoisin sauce

Instructions:

1. Gently heat the shredded leftover chicken.
2. Place a spoonful of chicken on each lettuce leaf.
3. Top with shredded carrots, chopped green onions, and a drizzle of hoisin sauce.
4. Fold the lettuce around the filling and enjoy as a light and tasty meal.

Orange Chicken Recipe with Fried Rice

Easy Eats

Prep Time:
20 minutes

Servings:
4-6

Ingredients:

- 1 lb boneless, skinless chicken breasts, cut into bite-sized pieces
- 1 cup cornstarch
- 2 eggs, beaten
- Salt and pepper to taste
- Vegetable oil for frying

For the Orange Sauce:

- 1 cup orange juice
- 1/4 cup soy sauce
- 1/2 cup brown sugar
- 1/4 cup rice vinegar
- 1 tablespoon grated ginger
- 2 garlic cloves, minced
- 1 tablespoon cornstarch, mixed with 2 tablespoons water
- Zest of 1 orange
- Red pepper flakes to taste (optional)

Instructions:

1. Season the chicken pieces with salt and pepper. Dredge them in cornstarch, then dip them in beaten eggs.
2. Heat vegetable oil in a deep pan over medium-high heat. Fry the chicken pieces until golden brown and cooked through. Drain on paper towels.
3. In a saucepan, combine orange juice, soy sauce, brown sugar, rice vinegar, grated ginger, and minced garlic. Bring to a simmer.
4. Stir in the cornstarch-water mixture and continue to cook until the sauce thickens.
5. Add the orange zest and red pepper flakes (if using). Mix well.
6. Toss the fried chicken pieces in the sauce until they are well coated.
7. Serve hot with fried rice and egg rolls (see Appetizers and Sides chapter for egg roll recipe)

Fried Rice Recipe

Ingredients:

- 2 cups cooked and cooled rice
- 2 tablespoons vegetable oil
- 1 small onion, chopped
- 1/2 cup frozen peas and carrots, thawed
- 2 eggs, lightly beaten
- 2 tablespoons soy sauce
- Salt and pepper to taste

Instructions:

1. Heat oil in a large skillet or wok over medium-high heat. Add onions and sauté until translucent.
2. Add peas and carrots, cooking until tender.
3. Push the vegetables to one side of the skillet. Pour the beaten eggs onto the other side and scramble.
4. Once the eggs are cooked, add the rice. Stir everything together.
5. Drizzle soy sauce over the rice and continue to stir-fry for a few minutes.
6. Season with salt and pepper to taste. Serve hot.

Orange Chicken Lettuce Wraps Using Leftovers

Prep Time:
20 minutes

Servings:
4-6

Ingredients:

- Leftover orange chicken, chopped
- 1 head of iceberg or butter lettuce, leaves separated
- 1 bell pepper, finely diced
- 1/2 cucumber, finely diced
- 1 carrot, grated
- 2 green onions, thinly sliced
- Fresh cilantro leaves, for garnish
- 2 tablespoons hoisin sauce
- 1 tablespoon soy sauce
- 1 teaspoon sesame oil
- Crushed peanuts, for garnish (optional)

Instructions:

1. In a small bowl, whisk together hoisin sauce, soy sauce, and sesame oil to create a dressing.
2. In a large mixing bowl, combine the chopped leftover orange chicken, bell pepper, cucumber, carrot, and green onions.
3. Pour the dressing over the chicken and vegetable mixture. Toss gently to coat everything evenly.
4. Take a lettuce leaf and place a spoonful of the orange chicken mixture in the center.
5. Garnish with fresh cilantro leaves and crushed peanuts if desired.
6. Fold the lettuce leaf around the filling and enjoy your refreshing and healthy lettuce wraps made from leftover orange chicken.

Easy Eats

Chicken Tikka Masala with Jasmine Rice, Chutney, Garlic Naan, and Creamed Spinach

Prep Time:
20 minutes

Servings:
4-6

Chicken Tikka Masala:
- 1 lb boneless, skinless chicken thighs, cut into chunks
- 1 cup plain yogurt
- 2 tbsp lemon juice
- 2 cloves garlic, minced
- 1 tbsp grated ginger
- 1 tbsp garam masala
- 1 tsp turmeric
- 1 tsp ground cumin
- 1 tsp paprika
- Salt and pepper to taste
- 2 tbsp vegetable oil
- 1 onion, finely chopped
- 1 can (14 oz) crushed tomatoes
- 1 cup heavy cream
- Fresh cilantro for garnish

Jasmine Rice:
- 1 cup jasmine rice
- 1 3/4 cups water
- Pinch of salt

Chutney:
- Store-bought or homemade mango chutney (see Sauces and Dips Chapter)

Garlic Naan:
- Store-bought or homemade garlic naan (see Appetizers and Sides Chapter)

Creamed Spinach:
- 1 lb fresh spinach
- 2 tbsp butter
- 2 cloves garlic, minced
- 1/2 cup heavy cream
- Salt and pepper to taste
- Nutmeg, a pinch

Instructions:

1. Marinate chicken: Combine yogurt, lemon juice, garlic, ginger, garam masala, turmeric, cumin, paprika, salt, and pepper. Coat chicken pieces in the marinade and refrigerate for at least 2 hours, preferably overnight.

2. Cook rice: Rinse jasmine rice until water runs clear. Combine rice, water, and a pinch of salt in a pot. Bring to a boil, then reduce heat to low, cover, and cook for 15-18 minutes until water is absorbed. Remove from heat and let it sit, covered, for 5 minutes.

3. For the masala sauce: Heat oil in a pan. Sauté onions until golden. Add the marinated chicken and cook until it's done. Add crushed tomatoes and simmer for 10 minutes. Stir in heavy cream and cook for another 5 minutes. Garnish with cilantro.

4. For creamed spinach: Sauté garlic in butter until fragrant. Add spinach and cook until wilted. Pour in heavy cream, season with salt, pepper, and a pinch of nutmeg. Cook until the cream thickens.

5. Serve hot chicken tikka masala with jasmine rice, a side of creamed spinach, garlic naan, and mango chutney.

Chicken Tikka Masala Wrap Using Leftovers

Prep Time:
20 minutes

Servings:
4-6

Ingredients:

- Leftover chicken tikka masala
- Flour tortillas
- Lettuce
- Sliced tomatoes
- Sliced onions
- Tzaziki (see Sauces and Dips Chapter)

Instructions:

1. Warm the flour tortillas.
2. Place lettuce, sliced tomatoes, and onions on each tortilla.
3. Add a generous amount of leftover chicken tikka masala.
4. Drizzle with cucumber yogurt sauce.
5. Roll up the tortillas to make wraps.
6. Serve and enjoy a delicious use of leftovers!

Now, let's create a black and white sketch of the Chicken Tikka Masala dinner with Jasmine Rice, Chutney, Garlic Naan, and Creamed Spinach.

Easy Eats

Chicken Curry with Broccoli Casserole Recipe

Prep Time:
20 minutes

Servings:
4-6

Ingredients:

- 4 chicken breasts, cooked and shredded
- 4 cups broccoli florets, blanched
- 1 cup mayonnaise
- 1 can cream of chicken soup
- 1 tablespoon lemon juice
- 2 teaspoons curry powder (adjust to taste)
- 1 cup shredded cheddar cheese
- 1/2 cup bread crumbs
- Salt and pepper to taste
- Chutney for serving
- Serve with homemade or bought Naan (see Sides) optional

Instructions:

1. Preheat your oven to 350°F (175°C).
2. In a large mixing bowl, combine the mayonnaise, cream of chicken soup, lemon juice, and curry powder. Mix well.
3. Add the shredded chicken and blanched broccoli to the curry mixture. Season with salt and pepper. Stir until everything is well coated.
4. Transfer the mixture to a greased casserole dish.
5. Sprinkle the top evenly with shredded cheddar cheese, followed by bread crumbs.
6. Bake for 25-30 minutes, or until the top is golden brown and the casserole is heated through.
7. Serve hot with chutney on the side.

Chicken Curry Broccoli Casserole Sandwiches Using Leftovers

Prep Time:
20 minutes

Servings:
4-6

Ingredients:

- Leftover chicken curry with broccoli casserole
- Bread slices
- Butter
- Cheddar cheese slices (optional)

Instructions:

1. Heat a skillet or griddle over medium heat.
2. Butter the outside of two slices of bread.
3. Place one slice of bread, buttered side down, on the skillet.
4. Add a slice of cheddar cheese (if using) on the bread.
5. Spoon a generous amount of leftover casserole on top of the cheese.
6. Top with another slice of bread, buttered side up.
7. Grill until the bottom bread is golden brown, then flip and grill the other side until golden and the cheese is melted.
8. Serve warm for a comforting and easy meal.

Easy Eats

Baked Chicken Breast Dinner with Corn and Carrots Recipe

Prep Time:
20 minutes

Servings:
4-6

Ingredients:

- 4 boneless, skinless chicken breasts
- 2 tbsp olive oil
- 1 tsp garlic powder
- 1 tsp paprika
- Salt and pepper, to taste
- 4 ears of corn, husked
- 4 large carrots, peeled and sliced

Instructions:

1. Preheat your oven to 375°F (190°C).
2. Rub the chicken breasts with olive oil, and season them with garlic powder, paprika, salt, and pepper.
3. Place the seasoned chicken breasts on a baking sheet.
4. Arrange the husked ears of corn and sliced carrots around the chicken on the baking sheet.
5. Bake in the preheated oven for 25-30 minutes or until the chicken is cooked through and the vegetables are tender.
6. Let the chicken rest for a few minutes before slicing. Serve the baked chicken breasts with the roasted corn and carrots.

Easy Eats

Chicken Pot Pie Recipe Using Leftovers

Prep Time:
20 minutes

Servings:
4-6

Ingredients:

- Leftover baked chicken breast, chopped
- Leftover corn, removed from the cob
- Leftover carrots, chopped
- 1/2 cup frozen peas
- 1/2 cup chopped onion
- 2 cloves garlic, minced
- 2 tbsp butter
- 2 tbsp all-purpose flour
- 1 cups chicken broth
- 1 8oz can of cream of mushroom soup
- Salt and pepper, to taste
- 1 sheet of puff pastry or pie crust, thawed

Instructions:

1. Preheat your oven to 400°F (200°C).
2. In a large skillet, melt butter over medium heat. Add onion and garlic, and sauté until translucent.
3. Stir in flour and cook for a minute.
4. Gradually add chicken broth and milk, stirring continuously until the sauce thickens.
5. Add the chopped leftover chicken, corn, carrots, and frozen peas to the skillet. Season with salt and pepper. Cook for a few minutes until everything is heated through.
6. Transfer the filling to a pie dish.
7. Cover the filling with a sheet of puff pastry or pie crust, trimming any excess. Make a few slits in the top for steam to escape.
8. Bake in the preheated oven for 25-30 minutes or until the crust is golden brown.
9. Let it cool for a few minutes before serving.

Enjoy this comforting chicken pot pie made with your delicious leftovers!

BBQ Chicken Thighs with Ranch Potato Bake and Wedge Salad

Prep Time:
20 minutes

Servings:
4-6

BBQ Chicken Thighs

Ingredients:

- 8 chicken thighs, skin on or skinless
- 1 cup BBQ sauce (see Sauces and Dips chapter)
- Salt and pepper to taste

Instructions:

1. Preheat Grill/Oven: Preheat your grill to medium-high heat or your oven to 375°F (190°C).
2. Season: Season the chicken thighs with salt and pepper.
3. Cook: Place the chicken thighs on the grill or in a baking dish if using an oven. Cook for about 25-30 minutes, turning occasionally, until the chicken is cooked through.
4. Glaze: During the last 10 minutes of cooking, brush the BBQ sauce over the chicken thighs, coating them evenly.
5. Serve: Once cooked, remove from heat and let rest for a few minutes before serving.

Ranch Potato Bake

Ingredients:

- 6 large potatoes, thinly sliced
- 1 cup sour cream
- 1 packet ranch seasoning
- 2 cups shredded cheddar cheese
- 6 slices cooked bacon, crumbled
- Salt and pepper to taste

Instructions:

1. Preheat Oven: Preheat your oven to 350°F (175°C).
2. Prepare Potatoes: Using a food processor or a knife, thinly slice the potatoes. Boil them in salted water until just tender, about 5-7 minutes. Drain well.
3. Make Ranch Sauce: In a bowl, mix together sour cream and ranch seasoning.
4. Layer: In a greased casserole dish, layer potatoes, ranch sauce, cheddar cheese, and crumbled bacon. Repeat the layers twice.
5. Bake: Cover with foil and bake for 25 minutes. Remove foil and bake for an additional 20 minutes or until the top is golden and bubbly.
6. Serve: Let it cool for a few minutes before serving.

Wedge Salad

Ingredients:

- 1 head iceberg lettuce, cut into 4 wedges
- 1 cup cherry tomatoes, halved
- 1/2 cup blue cheese dressing
- 1/4 cup crumbled blue cheese
- sprinkle with bacon bits
- Salt and pepper to taste

Instructions:

1. Assemble: Place each lettuce wedge on a plate. Drizzle with blue cheese dressing.
2. Add Toppings: Scatter cherry tomatoes and crumbled blue cheese and bacon over each wedge.
3. Season: Sprinkle with salt and pepper.
4. Serve: Serve immediately as a fresh side.

BBQ Chicken and Ranch Potato Casserole Using Leftovers

Prep Time: 20 minutes

Servings: 4-6

Ingredients:

- Leftover BBQ chicken thighs, shredded
- Leftover ranch potato bake
- 1 cup shredded cheese (optional)
- Chopped green onions or chives for garnish

Instructions:

1. Preheat Oven: Preheat your oven to 350°F (175°C).
2. Shred Chicken: Remove the bones and skin from the BBQ chicken thighs and shred the meat.
3. Layer: In a casserole dish, layer the shredded BBQ chicken at the bottom.
4. Add Potatoes: Spread the leftover ranch potato bake over the chicken.
5. Add Cheese: If desired, sprinkle an additional cup of shredded cheese on top.
6. Bake: Bake for 20-25 minutes or until everything is heated through and the cheese is melted.
7. Garnish: Sprinkle chopped green onions or chives on top for garnish.
8. Serve: Serve hot as a comforting and easy leftover meal.

Easy Eats

Stuffed Pork Tenderloin Dinner

Prep Time:
20 minutes

Servings:
4-6

Stuffed Pork Tenderloin
Ingredients:

- 1 pork tenderloin (about 1.5 lbs)
- 1 cup spinach, chopped
- 1/2 cup feta cheese, crumbled
- 1/4 cup sun-dried tomatoes, chopped
- 2 cloves garlic, minced
- 1 tbsp olive oil
- Salt and pepper to taste
- Kitchen twine

Instructions:

1. Preheat Oven: Preheat your oven to 375°F (190°C).
2. Prepare Filling: In a bowl, mix together spinach, feta cheese, sun-dried tomatoes, and minced garlic.
3. Butterfly Pork: Slice the pork tenderloin lengthwise, but not all the way through, so it opens like a book. Place it between two pieces of plastic wrap and pound it lightly with a meat mallet to even thickness.
4. Stuff and Roll: Spread the filling over the pork, leaving a small border around the edges. Roll the pork tightly and secure with kitchen twine.
5. Season: Rub the outside with olive oil, salt, and pepper.
6. Sear: In an oven-safe pan over medium-high heat, sear the pork on all sides until golden brown.
7. Bake: Transfer the pan to the oven and bake for 25-30 minutes, or until the internal temperature reaches 145°F (63°C).
8. Rest: Let the pork rest for 10 minutes, then remove the twine and slice.

Roasted Garlic Parmesan Asparagus
Ingredients:

- 1 lb asparagus, trimmed
- 2 tbsp olive oil
- 3 cloves garlic, minced
- 1/4 cup grated Parmesan cheese
- Salt and pepper to taste
- Lemon wedges for serving

Instructions:

1. Preheat Oven: Preheat your oven to 400°F (200°C).
2. Season Asparagus: Place asparagus on a baking sheet. Drizzle with olive oil, and sprinkle with minced garlic, Parmesan cheese, salt, and pepper.

3. Roast: Toss to coat evenly and spread in a single layer. Roast for 12-15 minutes, until tender and slightly crispy.
4. Serve: Serve the asparagus with lemon wedges on the side.

Herbed Couscous

Ingredients:

- 1 cup couscous
- 1 1/4 cups chicken or vegetable broth
- 2 tbsp butter
- 1/4 cup fresh parsley, chopped
- 1/4 cup fresh basil, chopped
- Salt and pepper to taste

Instructions:

1. Cook Couscous: In a saucepan, bring broth to a boil. Stir in couscous and butter. Remove from heat, cover, and let stand for 5 minutes.
2. Fluff and Season: Fluff couscous with a fork. Stir in chopped parsley, basil, salt, and pepper.
3. Serve: Serve warm as a flavorful and easy side.

These sides add a lovely balance of flavors and textures to the stuffed pork tenderloin, creating a satisfying and well-rounded meal.

Pork Tenderloin Sandwich Using Leftovers

Prep Time:
20 minutes

Servings:
4-6

Ingredients:

- Slices of leftover stuffed pork tenderloin
- 2 ciabatta rolls, halved
- 1/4 cup mayonnaise
- 1 tbsp Dijon mustard
- Lettuce leaves
- Tomato slices
- Salt and pepper to taste

Instructions:

1. Prepare Spread: In a small bowl, mix together mayonnaise and Dijon mustard.
2. Assemble Sandwiches: Spread the mayonnaise mixture on the ciabatta rolls. Place slices of leftover stuffed pork tenderloin on the bottom halves of the rolls.
3. Add Toppings: Add lettuce leaves and tomato slices on top of the pork. Season with salt and pepper.
4. Serve: Top with the other halves of the ciabatta rolls and serve immediately for a delicious and easy lunch using leftovers.

Stuffed Pork Chops with Garlic Mashed Potatoes and Honey Glazed Carrots

Prep Time:
20 minutes

Servings:
4-6

Ingredients:

- 4 pork chops, bone-in, about 1-inch thick
- 4 oz cream cheese, softened
- 1/2 cup spinach, chopped
- 1/4 cup sun-dried tomatoes, chopped
- 2 cloves garlic, minced
- 1/4 cup Parmesan cheese, grated
- Salt and pepper to taste
- 2 tbsp olive oil

Instructions:

1. Preheat Oven: Preheat oven to 375°F (190°C).
2. Prepare Filling: In a bowl, mix together cream cheese, spinach, sun- dried tomatoes, garlic, and Parmesan cheese. Season with salt and pepper.
3. Stuff Pork Chops: Cut a pocket into the side of each pork chop. Stuff each chop with the cream cheese mixture.
4. Season: Season the outside of the pork chops with salt and pepper.
5. Sear: Heat olive oil in an oven-safe skillet over medium-high heat. Sear pork chops for 2-3 minutes on each side.
6. Bake: Transfer the skillet to the oven and bake for 15-20 minutes, or until pork chops are cooked through.
7. Rest and Serve: Let the pork chops rest for a few minutes before serving.

Garlic Mashed Potatoes Recipe

Ingredients:

- 2 pounds of potatoes (preferably Yukon Gold), peeled and quartered
- 4 cloves of garlic, peeled
- 1/2 cup milk
- 1/4 cup heavy cream
- 4 tablespoons unsalted butter
- Salt and black pepper, to taste
- Fresh parsley, finely chopped (for garnish)

Instructions:

1. Place the peeled and quartered potatoes in a large pot. Add the whole garlic cloves. Fill the pot with enough water to cover the potatoes and bring to a boil over high heat.
2. Reduce the heat to medium and simmer the potatoes and garlic until they are fork-tender, about 15-20 minutes.

3. Drain the potatoes and garlic and return them to the pot. Add the butter and let it melt with the residual heat.
4. Using a potato masher or a hand mixer, mash the potatoes and garlic together until smooth.
5. Gradually add the milk and heavy cream, continuing to mash until the potatoes reach your desired consistency. If you prefer creamier mashed potatoes, add more milk as needed.
6. Season with salt and black pepper to taste.
7. Transfer the mashed potatoes to a serving bowl and garnish with chopped fresh parsley.
8. Serve warm as a comforting side dish.

Honey Glazed Carrots Recipe

Ingredients:

- 1 pound of carrots, peeled and sliced into 1/4 inch thick rounds
- 2 tablespoons unsalted butter
- 2 tablespoons honey
- Salt and black pepper, to taste
- Fresh parsley or thyme, finely chopped (for garnish)

Instructions:

1. In a large skillet, melt the butter over medium heat.
2. Add the sliced carrots to the skillet and sauté for about 5 minutes, or until they start to soften.
3. Drizzle the honey over the carrots and toss to coat evenly. Continue to cook for another 5-7 minutes, or until the carrots are tender and glazed.
4. Season with salt and black pepper to taste.
5. Garnish with chopped fresh parsley or thyme.
6. Serve hot as a sweet and savory side dish.

Creamy Pork Pasta Using Leftovers

Easy Eats

Prep Time:
20 minutes

Servings:
4-6

Ingredients:

- Leftover stuffed pork chops, chopped
- 8 oz pasta (e.g., penne or fettuccine)
- 1 cup heavy cream
- 1/2 cup chicken broth
- 1/4 cup Parmesan cheese, grated
- 2 cloves garlic, minced
- 1 tbsp olive oil
- Salt and pepper to taste
- Fresh parsley, chopped for garnish

Instructions:

1. Cook Pasta: Cook pasta according to package instructions. Drain and set aside.
2. Sauté Garlic: In a large skillet, heat olive oil over medium heat. Add minced garlic and sauté until fragrant.
3. Add Cream: Pour in heavy cream and chicken broth. Bring to a simmer.
4. Add Pork: Add chopped leftover pork chops to the skillet. Cook for a few minutes until heated through.
5. Combine: Add cooked pasta and Parmesan cheese to the skillet. Toss until pasta is coated in the creamy sauce.
6. Season: Season with salt and pepper to taste.
7. Serve: Garnish with fresh parsley and serve warm.

This creamy pork pasta is a delightful way to transform your leftover stuffed pork chops into a new and exciting meal.

Slow Cooker BBQ Baby Back Ribs with Pasta Salad and Potato Salad

Prep Time:
20 minutes

Servings:
4-6

BBQ Baby Back Ribs:

Ingredients:

- 2 racks of baby back ribs
- 1 tablespoon paprika
- 1 tablespoon garlic powder
- 1 tablespoon onion powder
- 1 tablespoon brown sugar
- 2 teaspoons salt
- 1 teaspoon black pepper
- 1 cup BBQ sauce (see Sauces and Dips chapter)

Instructions:

1. In a small bowl, mix together paprika, garlic powder, onion powder, brown sugar, salt, and pepper to create the dry rub.
2. Rub the mixture all over the ribs, making sure they are well-coated.
3. Cut each rack in half and place them in the slow cooker, stacking them if necessary.
4. Cover and cook on low for 6-7 hours or on high for 3-4 hours, until the ribs are tender.
5. Carefully remove the ribs from the slow cooker and place them on a baking sheet. Brush generously with BBQ sauce.
6. Broil in the oven for a few minutes until the sauce is caramelized and bubbly.
7. Serve hot with extra BBQ sauce on the side.

Pasta Salad:

Ingredients:

- 3 cups cooked pasta (e.g., fusilli, penne)
- 1 cup cherry tomatoes, halved
- 1 cucumber, diced
- 1/2 red onion, finely chopped
- 1/2 cup black olives, sliced
- 1/2 cup Italian dressing
- Salt and pepper, to taste
- Fresh basil leaves, for garnish

Instructions:

1. In a large bowl, combine cooked pasta, cherry tomatoes, cucumber, red onion, and black olives.
2. Pour Italian dressing over the salad and toss well to coat.
3. Season with salt and pepper to taste.
4. Garnish with fresh basil leaves.

5. Chill in the refrigerator until ready to serve.

Potato Salad:

Ingredients:

- 2 pounds potatoes, boiled and diced
- 4 boiled eggs, chopped
- 1/2 cup mayonnaise
- 2 tablespoons mustard
- 1/4 cup celery, finely chopped
- 1/4 cup pickles, chopped
- Salt and pepper, to taste
- Paprika, for garnish

Instructions:

1. In a large bowl, combine diced potatoes, chopped eggs, celery, and pickles.
2. In a separate bowl, mix together mayonnaise and mustard. Pour this over the potato mixture and gently stir to combine.
3. Season with salt and pepper to taste.
4. Sprinkle paprika on top for garnish.
5. Refrigerate for at least 1 hour before serving.

Leftover BBQ Rib Sandwiches

Prep Time:
20 minutes

Servings:
4-6

Ingredients:

- Leftover BBQ baby back ribs, meat removed from bones and shredded
- 4 sandwich rolls or buns
- Extra BBQ sauce
- 1 cup coleslaw (see Soups and Salads Chapter)
- Pickles, for serving

Instructions:

1. Heat the shredded rib meat in a pan with some extra BBQ sauce until warmed through.
2. Toast the sandwich rolls or buns.
3. Assemble the sandwiches by placing a generous amount of the warm BBQ rib meat on the bottom half of each roll.
4. Top with coleslaw and additional BBQ sauce if desired.
5. Serve with pickles on the side for a delicious and satisfying meal made from leftovers.

Slow Cooker Pulled Pork Recipe with Corn on the Cobb

Prep Time: 15 minutes | Cook Time: 8 hours | Total Time: 8 hours 15 minutes

Servings: 8

Ingredients

- 4-5 pounds pork shoulder or butt
- 1 large onion, sliced
- 4 cloves garlic, minced
- 1 cup chicken or beef broth
- 1 cup barbecue sauce (plus extra for serving)
- 2 tablespoons brown sugar
- 2 tablespoons apple cider vinegar
- 1 tablespoon smoked paprika
- 1 tablespoon mustard powder
- 1 tablespoon Worcestershire sauce
- 1 teaspoon chili powder
- Salt and pepper to taste
- Buns for serving

Instructions

1. Prepare Pork:
- Season the pork shoulder with salt and pepper. Rub the smoked paprika, mustard powder, and chili powder all over the pork.

2. Layer Slow Cooker:
- Place the sliced onion and miced garlic in the bottom of the slow cooker.

3. Combine Ingredients:
- In a bowl, mix together the barbecue sauce, brown sugar, apple cider vinegar, and Worcestershire sauce.

4. Cook:
- Place the seasoned pork on top of the onions and garlic in the slow cooker.
- Pour the sauce mixture and broth over the pork.
- Cover and cook on low for 8 hours, or until the pork is very tender.

5. Shred Pork:
- Remove the pork from the slow cooker and shred it using two forks.
- Skim off any excess fat from the liquid in the slow cooker.
- Return the shredded pork to the slow cooker and mix with the remaining juices.

6. Serve:
- Serve the pulled pork on buns with extra barbecue sauce, coleslaw, or your favorite toppings or on it's own with corn and salad.

Easy Eats

Corn on the Cob Ingredients:

- Fresh ears of corn on the cob (as many as you'd like to serve)
- Water for boiling
- Salt (optional)
- Butter (for serving)

Instructions:

1. Fill a large pot with enough water to cover the corn. Bring the water to a rolling boil over high heat.
2. While waiting for the water to boil, husk the corn, removing the outer green layers and silk. Rinse the corn under cold water to clean off any remaining silk or dirt.
3. Once the water is boiling, gently place the corn cobs in the pot. If you'd like, add a pinch of salt to the water.
4. Cover the pot with a lid and let the corn cook for 7-10 minutes, depending on how tender you like your corn. Avoid overcooking as it can make the corn tough.
5. Use tongs to remove the corn from the water and place it on a serving platter or dish.
6. Serve the corn hot, with butter on the side for spreading. You can also sprinkle additional salt, pepper, or other seasonings to taste.

Enjoy your boiled corn on the cob as a side dish, or even as a main attraction at a summer barbecue. It's delicious either way!

Pulled Pork Tacos Using Leftovers

Easy Eats

Prep Time: 10 minutes | Cook Time: 5 minutes | Total Time: 15 minutes

Servings: 4

Ingredients

- 2 cups leftover pulled pork
- 8 small corn or flour tortillas
- 1 cup shredded cabbage or coleslaw mix
- 1/2 cup diced tomatoes
- 1/2 cup diced red onion
- 1/4 cup chopped cilantro
- Lime wedges for serving
- Sour cream or avocado slices (optional)

Instructions

1. Reheat Pork:

- In a pan, gently reheat the leftover pulled pork until warm.

2. Prepare Toppings:

- While the pork is reheating, prepare your toppings: shred cabbage, dice tomatoes, dice red onion, and chop cilantro.

3. Warm Tortillas:

- Warm the tortillas in a dry skillet or in the microwave.

4. Assemble Tacos:

- Place a scoop of warm pulled pork on each tortilla.
- Top with shredded cabbage, diced tomatoes, red onion, and cilantro.

5. Serve:

- Serve the tacos with lime wedges for squeezing.
- Add sour cream or avocado slices if desired.

Enjoy a quick and delicious meal using your leftover pulled pork, perfect for a weeknight dinner!

Easy Eats

Slow Cooker Pork Chile Verde Recipe

Prep Time: 15 minutes | Cook Time: 8 hours | Total Time: 8 hours 15 minutes

Servings: 6-8

Ingredients

- 3 pounds pork shoulder, cut into cubes
- 1 pound tomatillos, husked and halved
- 2 poblano peppers, seeded and chopped
- 2 jalapeño peppers, seeded and chopped
- 1 large onion, chopped
- 4 garlic cloves, minced
- 2 cups chicken broth
- 1 tablespoon ground cumin
- 1 tablespoon dried oregano
- Salt and pepper to taste
- Fresh cilantro, chopped (for garnish)
- Lime wedges (for serving)

Instructions

1. Prepare Ingredients:
   - Season the pork cubes with salt, pepper, cumin, and oregano.

2. Layer Slow Cooker:
   - Place the tomatillos, poblano peppers, jalapeño peppers, onion, and garlic in the slow cooker.

3. Add Pork:
   - Add the seasoned pork on top of the vegetables.

4. Cook:
   - Pour the chicken broth over the pork and vegetables.
   - Cover and cook on low for 8 hours or until the pork is tender.

5. Blend Sauce:
   - Use an immersion blender or transfer the mixture to a blender. Blend until smooth.

6. Serve:
   - Return the blended sauce to the slow cooker and stir with the pork.
   - Garnish with fresh cilantro and serve with lime wedges.

Easy Eats

Pork Chile Verde Burrito with Black Beans, Rice, and Fried Eggs Using Leftovers

Prep Time: 20 minutes | Cook Time: 10 minutes | Total Time: 30 minutes

Servings: 4

Ingredients

- 4 large flour tortillas
- 2 cups leftover Pork Chile Verde, warmed
- 1 can black beans, drained and rinsed
- 2 cups cooked rice
- 1 cup shredded cheese (cheddar or Mexican blend)
- 4 eggs
- Salt and pepper to taste
- Optional toppings: sour cream, guacamole, salsa

Instructions

1. Prepare Burrito Filling:
- Warm the Pork Chile Verde in a pan over medium heat.
- Heat the black beans in a separate pan.

2. Cook Rice:
- If you don't have leftover rice, cook 1 cup of rice according to package instructions.

3. Assemble Burritos:
- Lay out the flour tortillas on a flat surface.
- Divide the rice and black beans evenly among the tortillas.
- Add a generous amount of Pork Chile Verde on top of the rice and beans.

4. Roll Burritos:
- Fold the sides of the tortilla over the filling, then roll tightly from bottom to top to form a burrito.

5. Melt Cheese:
- Place the burritos seam-side down in a baking dish.
- Sprinkle cheese over the top of the burritos.
- Broil in the oven until the cheese is melted and bubbly.

6. Fry Eggs:
- While the cheese is melting, fry the eggs to your desired doneness in a skillet.

7. Serve:
- Top each burrito with a fried egg.
- Serve with optional toppings like sour cream, guacamole, or salsa.

Enjoy a hearty and flavorful burrito that combines the deliciousness of Pork Chile Verde with the comfort of black beans, rice, and melted cheese, all topped with a perfectly fried egg!

Breaded Pork Chops, Homemade Macaroni and Cheese, and Green Beans

Prep Time:
20 minutes

Servings:
4-6

Ingredients:

- 4 pork chops
- 1 cup all-purpose flour + 4 tbsp for cheese sauce
- 2 eggs, beaten
- 2 cups breadcrumbs
- Salt and pepper to taste
- 1 lb macaroni pasta
- 4 cups shredded cheddar cheese
- 2 cups milk
- 4 tbsp butter
- 1 lb fresh green beans, trimmed
- 2 tbsp olive oil
- 1 clove garlic, minced

Instructions:

1. Breaded Pork Chops:

- Season pork chops with salt and pepper.
- Dredge each pork chop in flour, dip in beaten eggs, and coat with breadcrumbs.
- In a large skillet, heat oil over medium heat and fry pork chops until golden brown and cooked through, about 4 minutes per side. Set aside.

2. Homemade Macaroni and Cheese:

- Cook macaroni according to package instructions. Drain and set aside.
- In a saucepan, melt butter and flour over medium heat and stir until combined and bubbling slightly. Slowly add milk and bring to a simmer stirring frequently to prevent burning.
- Gradually add shredded cheddar cheese, stirring continuously until melted and smooth.
- Combine the cheese sauce with the cooked macaroni. Mix well and set aside.

3. Green Beans:

- In a skillet, heat olive oil over medium heat. Add minced garlic and green beans.
- Sauté for 5-7 minutes until green beans are tender but still crisp.
- Season with salt and pepper to taste.

Pork Chop Mac and Cheese Casserole Using Leftovers

Prep Time: 20 minutes

Servings: 4-6

Ingredients:

- Leftover breaded pork chops, chopped
- Leftover macaroni and cheese
- 1 cup of leftover green beans, chopped
- 1/2 cup breadcrumbs
- 2 tbsp melted butter

Instructions:

1. Preheat the oven to 350°F (175°C).
2. In a large mixing bowl, combine chopped pork chops, leftover macaroni and cheese, and green beans.
3. Transfer the mixture to a baking dish.
4. In a small bowl, mix breadcrumbs with melted butter, then sprinkle over the casserole.
5. Bake for 20-25 minutes, or until the top is golden and crispy.
6. Serve warm.

Easy Eats

Herb-Crusted Steak with Garlic Mashed Potatoes and Honey-Glazed Carrots

Prep Time:

20 minutes

Servings:

4-6

For the Herb-Crusted Steak:

- 2 ribeye or sirloin steaks (about 1-inch thick)
- 2 tbsp olive oil
- 2 cloves garlic, minced
- 1 tbsp fresh rosemary, finely chopped
- 1 tbsp fresh thyme, finely chopped
- Salt and freshly ground black pepper, to taste

For the Garlic Mashed Potatoes:

- 4 large potatoes, peeled and quartered
- 4 cloves garlic, peeled
- 1/2 cup milk or cream
- 4 tbsp unsalted butter
- Salt and pepper, to taste

For the Honey-Glazed Carrots:

- 4 large carrots, peeled and sliced diagonally
- 2 tbsp honey
- 2 tbsp butter
- Salt and pepper, to taste

Instructions:

1. Preparation for Steak:
- Preheat the grill or a skillet over medium-high heat.
- In a small bowl, mix olive oil, minced garlic, rosemary, thyme, salt, and pepper.
- Rub the herb mixture over both sides of the steaks.

2. Cooking the Steak:
- Grill or pan-sear the steaks to your preferred level of doneness (about 4-5 minutes per side for medium-rare).
- Once done, let the steaks rest for 5 minutes before slicing.

3. For the Garlic Mashed Potatoes:
- Place potatoes and garlic in a pot and cover with water. Bring to a boil and then reduce to a simmer. Cook until potatoes are tender.
- Drain the potatoes and return them to the pot. Add milk or cream, butter, and mash until smooth. Season with salt and pepper.

4. For the Honey-Glazed Carrots:
- In a skillet over medium heat, melt butter. Add carrots and cook for about 5-7 minutes.
- Add honey, salt, and pepper, and continue to cook until the carrots are tender and glazed.

5. Serving:
- Slice the rested steak and serve with a generous portion of garlic mashed potatoes and honey-glazed carrots on the side.

Enjoy a flavorful and satisfying dinner with perfectly cooked steak and delightful sides!

Steak and Eggs Skillet Breakfast Using Leftovers

Prep Time:
20 minutes

Servings:
4-6

Ingredients:

- Leftover steak, chopped into bite-sized pieces
- 4 large eggs
- 1 small onion, diced
- 1 bell pepper, diced
- 2 medium potatoes, diced
- 1/2 cup shredded cheese (cheddar or Monterey Jack)
- Salt and pepper, to taste
- 2 tbsp olive oil
- Fresh parsley or chives, chopped for garnish
- Hot sauce (optional)

Instructions:

1. Heat olive oil in a large skillet over medium heat.
2. Add the diced potatoes to the skillet and season with salt and pepper. Cook until they are golden and tender, stirring occasionally.
3. Add the diced onion and bell pepper to the skillet. Cook until the vegetables are softened.
4. Stir in the chopped leftover steak and cook for another 2-3 minutes, just to heat the steak through.
5. Make four wells in the mixture and crack an egg into each well.
6. Cover the skillet with a lid and cook until the egg whites are set but the yolks are still runny, or to your desired level of doneness.
7. Sprinkle shredded cheese over the top and cover for another minute to let the cheese melt.
8. Garnish with chopped parsley or chives, and serve hot with a dash of hot sauce if desired.

Enjoy a hearty and delicious breakfast skillet that makes the most of your leftover steak!

Easy Eats

Beef with Broccoli Recipe

Prep Time:
20 minutes

Servings:
4-6

Ingredients:

- 1 lb beef steak, thinly sliced
- 2 cups broccoli florets
- 3 tbsp soy sauce
- 2 tbsp oyster sauce
- 1 tbsp brown sugar
- 3 garlic cloves, minced
- 1 tbsp ginger, grated
- 1 tbsp cornstarch
- 1/2 cup beef broth or water
- 2 tbsp vegetable oil

For the Fried Rice:

- 2 cups cooked rice, chilled
- 2 eggs, beaten
- 1 cup mixed vegetables (peas, carrots, corn)
- 2 tbsp soy sauce
- 1 tbsp sesame oil
- 2 green onions, chopped
- Salt and pepper, to taste

Instructions:

1. **Marinate Beef:** In a bowl, combine soy sauce, oyster sauce, brown sugar, minced garlic, and grated ginger. Add the sliced beef and marinate for at least 15 minutes.
2. **Cook Broccoli:** In a pot of boiling water, blanch the broccoli florets for about 2 minutes. Drain and set aside.
3. **Cook Beef:** In a large skillet or wok, heat 1 tbsp of vegetable oil over high heat. Add the marinated beef and stir-fry until browned. Remove beef from the skillet.
4. **Make Sauce:** In the same skillet, add the beef broth or water and bring to a simmer. Mix cornstarch with a little water and add to the skillet to thicken the sauce.
5. **Combine:** Return the beef to the skillet. Add the broccoli and toss everything together until well coated with the sauce. Cook for an additional 2-3 minutes.
6. **Make Fried Rice:** In a separate skillet or wok, heat sesame oil. Add the beaten eggs and scramble. Add the chilled rice, mixed vegetables, and soy sauce. Stir-fry until everything is well combined and heated through. Season with salt and pepper. Garnish with chopped green onions.
7. **Serve:** Serve the beef with broccoli alongside the fried rice. Enjoy your delicious meal!

Easy Eats

Beef and Broccoli Stir-Fry Wraps Using Leftovers

Prep Time:
20 minutes

Servings:
4-6

Ingredients:

- Leftover beef with broccoli
- 4 large flour tortillas
- 2 tablespoons hoisin sauce
- 1 tablespoon soy sauce
- 1 tablespoon sesame oil
- 1 teaspoon garlic, minced
- 1 teaspoon ginger, minced
- 1 cup shredded carrots
- 1 cup bean sprouts
- 1 cup shredded cabbage
- 2 green onions, thinly sliced
- 1 tablespoon sesame seeds (optional)

Instructions:

1. Prepare the Stir-Fry Sauce: In a small bowl, whisk together the hoisin sauce, soy sauce, sesame oil, garlic, and ginger. Set aside.
2. Heat the Leftovers: In a large skillet or wok, gently reheat the leftover beef with broccoli over medium heat until warmed through.
3. Add Vegetables: Add the shredded carrots, bean sprouts, and cabbage to the skillet with the beef and broccoli. Stir-fry for 2-3 minutes until the vegetables are slightly softened but still crisp.
4. Combine with Sauce: Pour the prepared stir-fry sauce over the beef and vegetable mixture. Stir well to coat everything evenly. Cook for an additional 2 minutes.
5. Assemble the Wraps: Warm the flour tortillas in the microwave or on a skillet. Lay them flat and divide the beef and vegetable stir-fry mixture among the tortillas.
6. Add Toppings: Sprinkle green onions and sesame seeds (if using) over the filling.
7. Roll and Serve: Fold in the sides of each tortilla, then roll them up tightly to enclose the filling. Slice in half and serve immediately.

Enjoy this creative and delicious way to use your leftover beef with broccoli, transformed into satisfying wraps with fresh, crunchy vegetables and a flavorful sauce!

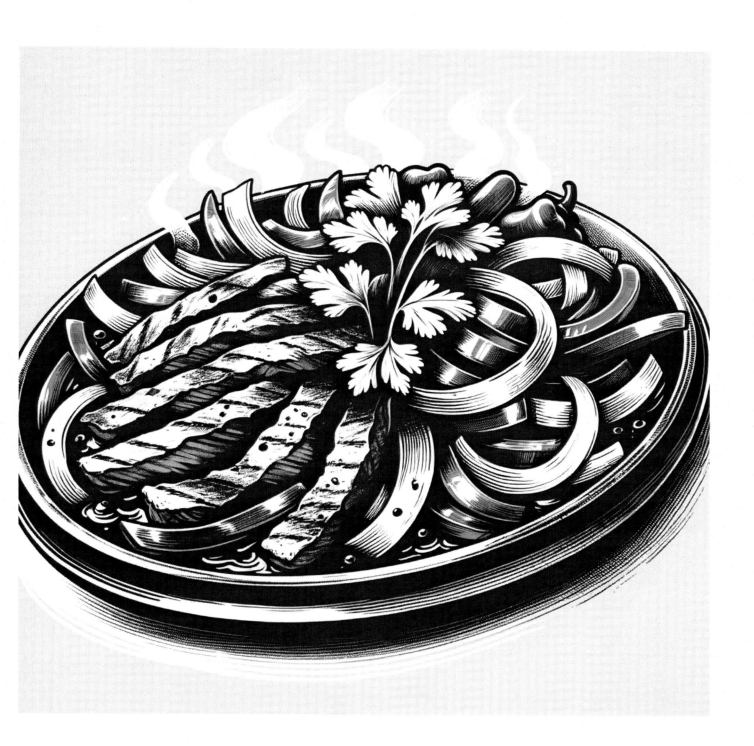

Easy Eats

Steak and Shrimp Fajitas Recipe

Prep Time: 20 minutes | Cook Time: 20 minutes | Total Time: 40 minutes

Servings: 4-6

Ingredients

- 1 pound flank steak, sliced into strips
- 1 pound large shrimp, peeled and deveined
- 3 bell peppers (red, yellow, green), sliced
- 1 large onion, sliced
- 3 tablespoons olive oil, divided
- Juice of 2 limes
- 3 garlic cloves, minced
- 2 teaspoons chili powder
- 2 teaspoons cumin
- 1 teaspoon paprika
- 1/2 teaspoon cayenne pepper (optional for heat)
- Salt and pepper to taste
- 8-10 flour tortillas, warmed
- Optional toppings: guacamole, sour cream, shredded cheese, salsa

Instructions

1. Marinate Steak and Shrimp:
   - In a large bowl, combine the lime juice, 2 tablespoons olive oil, minced garlic, chili powder, cumin, paprika, cayenne pepper, salt, and pepper.
   - Add the sliced steak and shrimp to the marinade. Toss to coat evenly.
   - Let the steak and shrimp marinate for at least 15 minutes.

2. Cook Vegetables:
   - Heat 1 tablespoon of olive oil in a large skillet over medium-high heat.
   - Add the sliced bell peppers and onion. Cook, stirring occasionally, until the vegetables are tender and slightly charred. Remove from skillet and set aside.

3. Cook Steak:
   - In the same skillet, add the marinated steak strips.
   - Cook for about 5-7 minutes or until the steak is cooked to your desired doneness. Remove from skillet and set aside.

4. Cook Shrimp:
   - In the same skillet, add the marinated shrimp.
   - Cook for 2-3 minutes on each side or until the shrimp are pink and opaque. Be careful not to overcook.

5. Assemble Fajitas:
   - On a warm tortilla, lay a portion of the cooked steak, shrimp, and sautéed

vegetables.
- Add your favorite toppings such as guacamole, sour cream, shredded cheese, or salsa.

6. Serve:
- Serve the fajitas hot with lime wedges for squeezing over the top.

Enjoy a sizzling platter of Shrimp and Steak Fajitas, bursting with vibrant flavors and colors, and customizable with a variety of toppings for a delightful dining experience!

Fajita Breakfast Hash Recipe Using Leftovers

Prep Time: 10 minutes | Cook Time: 20 minutes | Total Time: 30 minutes

Servings: 4

Ingredients

- Leftover shrimp and steak from fajitas, chopped
- Leftover sautéed bell peppers and onions
- 2 cups diced potatoes
- 4 large eggs
- 1/2 cup shredded cheese (your choice)
- 2 tablespoons olive oil
- Salt and pepper, to taste
- Chopped fresh cilantro for garnish
- Optional: hot sauce or salsa for serving

Instructions

1. Prepare Potatoes:

- In a large skillet, heat 1 tablespoon of olive oil over medium heat.
- Add the diced potatoes, season with salt and pepper, and cook until they are golden and crispy, about 10-15 minutes. Stir occasionally to ensure even cooking.

2. Add Fajita Leftovers:

- Add the chopped leftover shrimp, steak, and sautéed vegetables to the skillet with the potatoes. Cook for another 5 minutes until everything is heated through.

3. Cook Eggs:

- Make four wells in the hash mixture and crack an egg into each well.
- Cover the skillet and cook until the eggs are done to your liking (about 4-6 minutes for soft yolks).

4. Add Cheese:

- Sprinkle shredded cheese over the hash and cover for a minute to let the cheese melt.

5. Serve:

- Garnish with chopped cilantro.
- Serve hot with optional hot sauce or salsa on the side.

This Fajita Leftover Breakfast Hash is a hearty and delicious way to start your day, repurposing your fajita leftovers into a flavorful and satisfying meal. Enjoy!

Meatloaf with Mashed Potatoes and Peas Recipe

Prep Time: 20 minutes | Cook Time: 1 hour | Total Time: 1 hour 20 minutes

Servings: 6

Meatloaf Ingredients

- 2 lbs ground beef
- 1 package dry onion soup mix
- 1/2 cup ketchup
- 1 large egg, beaten
- 3/4 cup breadcrumbs Mashed Potatoes Ingredients
- 4 large potatoes, peeled and quartered
- 1/4 cup milk
- 2 tablespoons butter
- Salt and pepper, to taste Peas Ingredients
- 2 cups frozen peas
- 1 tablespoon butter
- Salt and pepper, to taste Meatloaf

Instructions

1. Preheat Oven:
- Preheat your oven to 350°F (175°C).

2. Mix Ingredients:
- In a large bowl, combine the ground beef, dry onion soup mix, ketchup, beaten egg, and breadcrumbs. Mix well.

3. Shape Meatloaf:
- Press the mixture into a loaf shape and place it in a lightly greased baking dish.

4. Bake:
- Bake in the preheated oven for 1 hour or until the meatloaf is cooked through.

Mashed Potatoes Instructions

1. Cook Potatoes:
- Place the quartered potatoes in a pot and cover with water. Bring to a boil and cook until tender, about 20 minutes.

2. Mash Potatoes:
- Drain the potatoes and return them to the pot. Add milk, butter, salt, and pepper. Mash until smooth and creamy.

Peas Instructions

1. Cook Peas:
- In a small saucepan, cook the frozen peas with a tablespoon of butter, salt, and pepper over medium heat until heated through, about 5-7 minutes.

Serve the meatloaf slices with a side of creamy mashed potatoes and buttered peas for a comforting and hearty meal.

Easy Eats

Meatloaf Sandwich Recipe Using Leftovers

Prep Time: 10 minutes | Cook Time: 5 minutes | Total Time: 15 minutes

Servings: 4

Ingredients

- Leftover meatloaf, sliced
- 8 slices of bread
- 4 tablespoons mayonnaise
- Lettuce leaves
- Tomato slices
- Optional: mustard or additional ketchup

Instructions

1. Prepare Sandwich:
- Toast the bread slices.
- Spread mayonnaise on one side of each slice of toasted bread.

2. Assemble Sandwich:
- Place a slice of meatloaf on the mayo-spread side of 4 bread slices.
- Add lettuce and tomato slices on top of the meatloaf.
- Add mustard or additional ketchup if desired.

3. Complete Sandwich:
- Top with the remaining slices of bread, mayo side down.

4. Serve:
- Cut the sandwiches in half and serve immediately.

Enjoy a delicious and easy Meatloaf Sandwich, a perfect way to use up leftover meatloaf and create a satisfying meal.

Slow Cooker Pot Roast with Sourdough Rolls

Prep Time: 20 minutes

Servings: 4-6

Ingredients:

- 3 lbs beef chuck roast
- 1 onion, sliced
- 4 carrots, peeled and chopped
- 4 potatoes, peeled and chopped
- 3 cloves garlic, minced
- 2 cups beef broth
- 1 tablespoon Worcestershire sauce
- 1 teaspoon dried rosemary
- 1 teaspoon dried thyme
- Salt and pepper to taste
- Sourdough rolls for serving

Instructions:

1. Season the chuck roast with salt and pepper on all sides.
2. In the slow cooker, place the sliced onion, chopped carrots, and potatoes at the bottom.
3. Place the seasoned chuck roast on top of the vegetables.
4. Add minced garlic, Worcestershire sauce, dried rosemary, and thyme.
5. Pour beef broth over the roast and vegetables.
6. Cover and cook on low for 8 hours or on high for 4-5 hours, until the meat is tender and falls apart easily.
7. Once cooked, shred the beef in the slow cooker and mix it with the vegetables and juices.
8. Serve hot with warm sourdough rolls on the side.

Pot Roast Pie Using Leftovers

Prep Time:
20 minutes

Servings:
4-6

Ingredients:

- Leftover pot roast (beef and vegetables), shredded
- 1 cup frozen peas
- 1 cup beef gravy (can use leftover juices from the pot roast)
- 1 sheet of puff pastry, thawed
- 1 egg, beaten for egg wash

Instructions:

1. Preheat the oven to 375°F (190°C).
2. In a large mixing bowl, combine the shredded leftover pot roast (beef and vegetables) with frozen peas and beef gravy. Mix well.
3. Pour the mixture into a pie dish or a deep baking dish.
4. Roll out the puff pastry to cover the top of the pie dish. Trim any excess pastry.
5. Crimp the edges of the pastry to seal the pie.
6. Brush the top of the pastry with beaten egg for a golden finish.
7. Make a few slits in the top of the pastry to allow steam to escape.
8. Bake for 30-35 minutes, or until the pastry is puffed and golden brown.
9. Let it cool for a few minutes before serving.

Enjoy the comforting flavors of the slow cooker pot roast with sourdough rolls for dinner and repurpose the leftovers into a delicious pot roast pie for the next meal!

Easy Eats

Shepard's Pie Recipe

Prep Time:
20 minutes

Servings:
4-6

Ingredients:

- 1 lb ground beef or lamb
- 1 onion, finely chopped
- 2 carrots, diced
- 2 cloves garlic, minced
- 1 cup frozen peas
- 2 tbsp tomato paste
- 1 tbsp Worcestershire sauce
- 1 cup beef or chicken broth
- Salt and pepper, to taste
- 3 cups mashed potatoes (prepared in advance)
- 1/2 cup grated cheddar cheese
- Sourdough rolls

Instructions:

1. Preheat your oven to 375°F (190°C).
2. In a large skillet, cook the ground beef or lamb over medium heat until browned. Drain excess fat.
3. Add the chopped onion, diced carrots, and minced garlic to the skillet. Cook until the vegetables are softened, about 5 minutes.
4. Stir in the frozen peas, tomato paste, Worcestershire sauce, and broth. Bring to a simmer and cook until slightly thickened, about 10 minutes. Season with salt and pepper.
5. Transfer the meat and vegetable mixture to a 9x13 inch baking dish.
6. Spread the mashed potatoes evenly over the top. Sprinkle with grated cheddar cheese.
7. Bake in the preheated oven for 20-25 minutes, or until the top is golden brown and the edges are bubbly.
8. Serve hot with warm dinner rolls.

Easy Eats

Shepard's Pie Stuffed Rolls Recipe Using Leftovers

Prep Time:
20 minutes

Servings:
4-6

Ingredients:

- Leftover Shepard's Pie
- Additional sourdough dinner rolls
- 1/4 cup melted butter
- 1 tsp garlic powder
- 1 tsp parsley flakes

Instructions:

1. Preheat your oven to 350°F (175°C).
2. Take the leftover Shepard's Pie and mix it well so the meat, vegetables, and mashed potatoes are combined.
3. Cut the top of each dinner roll and hollow out the inside slightly.
4. Stuff each roll with the Shepard's Pie mixture.
5. In a small bowl, mix the melted butter with garlic powder and parsley flakes.
6. Brush the stuffed rolls with the garlic butter mixture.
7. Place the stuffed rolls on a baking sheet and bake for 10-15 minutes, or until the rolls are heated through and slightly crispy.
8. Serve warm as a delicious snack or light meal.

Classic Lasagna Recipe

Easy Eats

Prep Time:
20 minutes

Servings:
4-6

Ingredients:

- 12 lasagna noodles
- 1 pound ground beef
- 1 medium onion, chopped
- 2 cloves garlic, minced
- 1 jar (24 ounces) marinara sauce
- 1 can (6 ounces) tomato paste
- 1 teaspoon dried oregano
- 1 teaspoon dried basil
- Salt and pepper to taste
- 2 cups ricotta cheese
- 1 egg, beaten
- 1/4 cup grated Parmesan cheese
- 3 cups shredded mozzarella cheese

Instructions:

1. Preheat your oven to 375°F (190°C).
2. Cook lasagna noodles according to package instructions, then drain and set aside.
3. In a large skillet, cook ground beef, onion, and garlic over medium heat until meat is no longer pink. Drain excess grease.
4. Stir in marinara sauce, tomato paste, oregano, basil, salt, and pepper. Bring to a simmer, then reduce heat and let it simmer for 10 minutes.
5. In a bowl, mix together ricotta cheese, beaten egg, and Parmesan cheese.
6. In a 9x13 inch baking dish, spread a thin layer of the meat sauce.
7. Layer with 3 noodles, followed by a third of the ricotta mixture, a third of the remaining meat sauce, and a third of the mozzarella cheese.
8. Repeat layers twice more.
9. Cover with aluminum foil and bake for 25 minutes. Remove foil and bake for an additional 25 minutes or until hot and bubbly.
10. Let stand for 10 minutes before serving.

Garlic Bread Ingredients:

- 1 baguette or French bread
- 1/2 cup unsalted butter, softened
- 3 cloves garlic, minced
- 2 tablespoons chopped parsley
- Salt to taste

Instructions:

1. Preheat your oven to 400°F (200°C).
2. Cut the baguette in half lengthwise.

3. In a small bowl, mix together butter, garlic, parsley, and salt.
4. Spread the garlic butter mixture evenly on the cut sides of the bread.
5. Place the bread on a baking sheet, cut side up, and bake for 10-12 minutes or until golden and crispy.

Simple Salad Ingredients:

- Mixed salad greens
- Cherry tomatoes, halved
- Cucumber, sliced
- Red onion, thinly sliced
- Your choice of salad dressing

Instructions:

1. In a large bowl, combine salad greens, cherry tomatoes, cucumber, and red onion.
2. Toss with your favorite salad dressing just before serving.

Serve the lasagna with warm garlic bread and a fresh side salad for a complete and satisfying meal.

Lasagna Soup with Garlic Bread Croutons Using Leftovers

Prep Time:
20 minutes

Servings:
4-6

Ingredients:

- Leftover lasagna, cut into bite-sized pieces (about 2 cups)
- 4 cups chicken or vegetable broth
- 1 can (14.5 ounces) diced tomatoes, undrained
- 1 onion, chopped
- 2 cloves garlic, minced
- 1 teaspoon Italian seasoning
- Salt and pepper to taste
- Olive oil
- Leftover garlic bread, cut into cubes
- Grated Parmesan cheese (optional)

Instructions:

1. In a large pot, heat a little olive oil over medium heat. Add the chopped onion and minced garlic, sautéing until the onion is translucent.
2. Add the diced tomatoes, chicken or vegetable broth, Italian seasoning, salt, and pepper. Bring the mixture to a boil.
3. Reduce heat to a simmer and add the leftover lasagna pieces. Stir gently to combine.
4. Let the soup simmer for about 10-15 minutes, or until everything is heated through and the flavors have melded.
5. While the soup is simmering, make the garlic bread croutons. Preheat your oven to 375°F (190°C).
6. Spread the garlic bread cubes on a baking sheet in a single layer. Drizzle with a little olive oil.
7. Bake for 5-10 minutes, or until the croutons are crispy and golden brown.
8. Serve the lasagna soup hot, garnished with garlic bread croutons and a sprinkle of grated Parmesan cheese, if desired.

This creative and comforting recipe is a great way to enjoy the flavors of lasagna in a new and exciting way, making the most out of your leftovers.

Jambalaya Recipe

Prep Time:
20 minutes

Servings:
4-6

Ingredients:

- 2 tablespoons olive oil
- 1 pound boneless, skinless chicken breasts, cut into bite-sized pieces
- 1 pound andouille sausage, sliced
- 1 pound shrimp, peeled and deveined
- 1 large onion, diced
- 1 bell pepper, diced
- 3 stalks celery, diced
- 4 cloves garlic, minced
- 2 cups long-grain rice
- 1 (14.5 oz) can diced tomatoes, with juice
- 4 cups chicken broth
- 2 teaspoons Cajun seasoning
- 1 teaspoon dried thyme
- 1/2 teaspoon paprika
- 1/2 teaspoon cayenne pepper (optional, for heat)
- Salt and pepper to taste
- 2 green onions, sliced (for garnish)

Instructions:

1. Heat olive oil in a large pot over medium-high heat. Add chicken and sausage, cook until browned. Remove and set aside.
2. In the same pot, add onion, bell pepper, celery, and garlic. Sauté until vegetables are tender.
3. Stir in rice, cook for 2 minutes.
4. Add diced tomatoes, chicken broth, Cajun seasoning, thyme, paprika, and cayenne pepper. Bring to a boil.
5. Reduce heat to low, cover, and simmer for 20 minutes.
6. Return chicken and sausage to the pot. Add shrimp. Cook until shrimp are pink and rice is tender, about 5-10 minutes.
7. Season with salt and pepper. Garnish with green onions.
8. Serve hot and enjoy!

Jambalaya Stuffed Peppers Recipe Using Leftovers

Prep Time:
20 minutes

Servings:
4-6

Ingredients:

- 4 large bell peppers, tops cut off and seeds removed
- 2 cups leftover jambalaya
- 1 cup shredded cheddar cheese
- 1/4 cup chicken broth
- Salt and pepper to taste
- Chopped parsley (for garnish)

Instructions:

1. Preheat oven to 350°F (175°C).
2. Arrange bell peppers in a baking dish. Season the insides with salt and pepper.
3. Spoon leftover jambalaya into each bell pepper. Press down gently to pack.
4. Pour chicken broth into the bottom of the baking dish. This will help keep the peppers moist while baking.
5. Cover the dish with aluminum foil and bake for 30 minutes.
6. Remove foil, top each pepper with shredded cheese, and bake for an additional 10 minutes or until cheese is melted and bubbly.
7. Garnish with chopped parsley.
8. Serve warm as a flavorful and unique way to enjoy your jambalaya leftovers!

Ground Beef Taco Recipe

Prep Time:
20 minutes

Servings:
4-6

Ingredients:

- 1 lb ground beef
- 1 packet taco seasoning
- Taco shells or tortillas
- Shredded cheese (cheddar or Mexican blend)
- Diced tomatoes
- Sliced black olives
- Shredded lettuce
- Diced onion
- Guacamole (see Sauces and Dips)
- Sour Cream
- Hot sauce (optional)

For the Sides:

- Cooked pinto beans
- Cooked rice

Instructions:

1. In a skillet over medium heat, brown the ground beef until fully cooked. Drain excess fat.
2. Add the taco seasoning to the beef, following the packet instructions (usually involves adding water).
3. Cook until the seasoning is well incorporated and the mixture has thickened.
4. Warm the taco shells or tortillas in the oven or on a skillet.
5. Assemble the tacos: Fill each shell or tortilla with the seasoned ground beef. Top with cheese, tomatoes, olives, lettuce, onion, and guacamole and sour cream. Add hot sauce if desired.
6. Serve the tacos with a side of pinto beans and rice.

Taco Soup Recipe Using Leftovers

Easy Eats

Prep Time:
20 minutes

Servings:
4-6

Ingredients:

- Leftover taco meat
- 1 can diced tomatoes
- 1 can corn, drained
- Leftover pinto beans
- Leftover rice
- 4 cups chicken or beef broth
- 1 packet taco seasoning (or leftover seasoning from tacos)
- Fritos for topping

Instructions:

1. In a large pot, combine the leftover taco meat, diced tomatoes, corn, black beans, pinto beans, broth, and taco seasoning.
2. Bring to a boil, then reduce heat and let simmer for 20-30 minutes, stirring occasionally.
3. Taste and adjust seasoning if needed.
4. Serve hot, topped with Fritos for added crunch, sour cream and guacamole.

Enjoy your delicious taco meal and the comforting soup made from the leftovers!

Homemade Spaghetti and Meatballs with Sauce

Prep Time:
20 minutes

Servings:
4-6

Ingredients:

For the Meatballs:

- 1 pound ground beef
- 1/2 pound ground pork (optional, can use all beef)
- 1/2 cup breadcrumbs
- 1/4 cup milk
- 1/4 cup grated Parmesan cheese
- 1 egg
- 2 cloves garlic, minced
- 1/4 cup fresh parsley, chopped
- Salt and pepper to taste
- 2 tablespoons olive oil, for frying

For the Sauce:

- 2 cans (14.5 ounces each) crushed tomatoes
- 1 can (6 ounces) tomato paste
- 4 cloves garlic, minced
- 1 medium onion, finely chopped
- 2 tablespoons olive oil
- 1 teaspoon sugar (optional, to cut acidity)
- 1 tablespoon dried basil
- 1 teaspoon dried oregano
- Salt and pepper to taste
- Red pepper flakes to taste (optional)
- Fresh basil leaves, for garnish

For the Pasta:

- 1 pound spaghetti
- Salt, for pasta water

Instructions:

1. **Prep the Meatballs:**
   - In a large bowl, soak the breadcrumbs in milk for 5 minutes.
   - Add the ground beef, ground pork, grated Parmesan, egg, minced garlic, parsley, and a good pinch of salt and pepper.
   - Mix until just combined; do not overmix. Form into 1½-inch meatballs.

2. **Brown the Meatballs:**
   - In a large skillet, heat 2 tablespoons of olive oil over medium-high heat.
   - Add meatballs in batches, being careful not to overcrowd the pan. Brown them on all sides, then remove

and set aside.

3. Make the Sauce:
   - In the same skillet, add 2 tablespoons of olive oil.
   - Sauté the onion until translucent, then add the minced garlic and cook until fragrant.
   - Stir in the crushed tomatoes and tomato paste. Add sugar, if using, to reduce acidity.
   - Season with dried basil, oregano, salt, pepper, and red pepper flakes.
   - Bring to a simmer, then reduce the heat to low.

4. Cook the Meatballs in Sauce:
   - Add the browned meatballs to the sauce. Cover and let simmer for about 30 minutes, or until the meatballs are cooked through.

5. Cook the Spaghetti:
   - While the sauce simmers, bring a large pot of salted water to a boil.
   - Cook the spaghetti according to the package instructions until al dente.
   - Drain and set aside, reserving some pasta water to loosen the sauce if necessary.

6. Serve:
   - Plate the spaghetti and top with meatballs and sauce.
   - Garnish with fresh basil leaves and extra grated Parmesan cheese if desired.

Notes:

- For a quicker weeknight meal, feel free to substitute the homemade sauce with a jar of your favorite store-bought sauce. Simply brown the meatballs as instructed, then simmer them in the store-bought sauce.
- The meatball mixture can also be used to make a meatloaf or mini meatloaf muffins if you have leftovers.
- Homemade sauce always tastes better the longer it simmers, so feel free to make the sauce ahead of time and let it simmer on low for a couple of hours, stirring occasionally.

Enjoy your meal of classic homemade spaghetti and meatballs, a comforting and hearty dish that's perfect for any day of the week!

Easy Eats

Meatball Sub Casserole Using Leftovers

Prep Time:
20 minutes

Servings:
4-6

Ingredients:

- Leftover spaghetti and meatballs (6-8 meatballs with sauce)
- 1 baguette or Italian loaf, cut into 1-inch thick slices
- 2 cups mozzarella cheese, shredded
- 1/2 cup grated Parmesan cheese
- 1 teaspoon Italian seasoning
- 1 tablespoon fresh basil, chopped (optional)
- 2 tablespoons olive oil
- 1 garlic clove, minced (for garlic oil)
- Additional fresh parsley or basil for garnish

Instructions:

1. Prepare Garlic Oil:
- In a small bowl, mix together the olive oil and minced garlic. Set aside to infuse for a few minutes.

2. Preheat the Oven:
- Preheat your oven to 375°F (190°C).

3. Prep the Bread:
- Brush each slice of baguette with the garlic oil on both sides and place them in a single layer on a baking tray.
- Toast in the preheated oven for about 5 minutes, or until slightly crispy but not completely hard.

4. Chop the Leftovers:
- Cut the leftover meatballs into slices.

5. Layer the Casserole:
- In a casserole dish, lay out the toasted bread slices, slightly overlapping.
- Spoon over the leftover meatball slices and sauce evenly across the bread.
- Sprinkle with Italian seasoning.

6. Add the Cheese:
- Cover the sauce and meatballs with the mozzarella cheese, then sprinkle over with the grated Parmesan.

7. Bake the Casserole:
- Cover with aluminum foil and bake in the oven for 20 minutes.
- After 20 minutes, remove the foil and bake for an additional 10 minutes or until the cheese is melted and bubbly.

8. Garnish and Serve:

- Once baked, let the casserole cool for a few minutes before garnishing with fresh basil or parsley.
- Cut into portions and serve as a hearty meatball sub in a dish.

Notes:

- The garlic oil adds a nice touch to the bread, but if you're short on time, you can skip this step and use the baguette as is.
- For an extra cheesy casserole, mix some ricotta with an egg and layer it over the bread before adding the meatball slices and sauce.
- If you prefer a little heat, sprinkle some crushed red pepper flakes on top before baking.

This Meatball Sub Casserole is a fun twist on a classic sandwich and a perfect way to use your leftovers for a cozy family dinner. Enjoy!

Easy Eats

Basil Shrimp Pasta

Prep Time:
20 minutes

Servings:
4-6

Ingredients:

For the Pasta:

- 1 lb linguine or spaghetti
- 1 lb shrimp, peeled and deveined
- 2 tablespoons olive oil
- 4 cloves garlic, minced
- 1/2 cup pesto (see Sauces and Dips chapter for the recipe)
- Salt and pepper, to taste
- Fresh basil leaves, for garnish
- Grated Parmesan cheese, for serving

For the Garlic Bread:

- 1 baguette or loaf of Italian bread, sliced in half lengthwise
- 4 tablespoons butter, softened
- 2 cloves garlic, minced
- 2 tablespoons fresh parsley,
- chopped Salt, to taste

For the Caesar Salad:

- 6 cups romaine lettuce, chopped
- 1/2 cup Caesar dressing
- 1/4 cup Parmesan cheese, grated
- 1 cup croutons

Instructions:

For the Basil Shrimp Pasta:

1. Cook the Pasta: Bring a large pot of salted water to a boil. Cook the pasta according to package instructions until al dente. Drain and set aside.
2. Cook the Shrimp: In a large skillet, heat olive oil over medium heat. Add garlic and sauté for 1 minute. Add shrimp, season with salt and pepper, and cook until the shrimp are pink and opaque, about 3-4 minutes per side.
3. Combine Pasta and Pesto: In a large bowl, toss the cooked pasta with the pesto sauce (see Sauces and Dips chapter for the recipe). Add the cooked shrimp and toss gently to combine.
4. Serve: Garnish with fresh basil leaves and grated Parmesan cheese.

For the Garlic Bread:

1. Preheat the Oven: Preheat your oven to 350°F (175°C). Prepare Garlic Butter: In a small bowl, combine the softened butter, minced garlic, chopped parsley, and salt.

2. Apply to Bread: Spread the garlic butter evenly on the cut sides of the bread.
3. Bake: Place the bread on a baking sheet and bake for 10-15 minutes, or until the edges are golden and crispy.

For the Caesar Salad:

1. Toss the Salad: In a large bowl, combine the chopped romaine lettuce, Caesar dressing, grated Parmesan cheese, and croutons.
2. Mix Well: Toss the salad until the lettuce is well coated with the dressing.
3. Serve: Plate the Basil Shrimp Pasta alongside a portion of Garlic Bread and a serving of Caesar Salad for a complete and satisfying meal.

Enjoy your delicious creation!

Easy Eats

Creamy Basil Shrimp Fritatta with Caesar Salad Croutons Using Leftovers

Prep Time:
20 minutes

Servings:
4-6

Ingredients:

- Leftover basil shrimp pasta
- 6 large eggs
- 1/4 cup milk or cream
- Salt and pepper to taste
- 1 tablespoon olive oil
- Leftover garlic bread, cut into small cubes
- Leftover Caesar salad (lettuce and Parmesan cheese)
- Additional grated Parmesan cheese for topping

Instructions:

1. Preheat Oven: Preheat your oven to 375°F (190°C).
2. Prepare the Shrimp Pasta: Roughly chop the leftover basil shrimp pasta into smaller pieces for easier incorporation into the frittata.
3. Make the Egg Mixture: In a large bowl, whisk together the eggs, milk or cream, salt, and pepper. Stir in the chopped basil shrimp pasta.
4. Cook the Frittata: Heat olive oil in an oven-safe skillet over medium heat. Pour the egg and shrimp pasta mixture into the skillet. Cook for about 5 minutes, or until the edges begin to set.
5. Bake the Frittata: Transfer the skillet to the preheated oven and bake for 15-20 minutes, or until the frittata is set and lightly golden on top.
6. Make Caesar Salad Croutons: While the frittata is baking, toss the cubes of leftover garlic bread with a bit of olive oil and spread them on a baking sheet. Bake in the oven for about 5-10 minutes, or until crispy and golden.
7. Serve: Remove the frittata from the oven and let it cool slightly. Top with leftover Caesar salad lettuce, additional grated Parmesan cheese, and the crispy Caesar salad croutons.
8. Slice and Enjoy: Slice the creamy basil shrimp frittata into wedges and serve warm. Enjoy this delightful and inventive meal made from your leftovers!

Tilapia Dinner with Baked Potato and Broccoli

Prep Time:
20 minutes

Servings:
4-6

Ingredients:

- 4 tilapia fillets
- 2 tablespoons olive oil
- 1 teaspoon garlic powder
- 1 teaspoon paprika
- Salt and pepper, to taste
- 4 large baking potatoes
- 1 head of broccoli, cut into florets
- Butter, sour cream, and chives for the baked potatoes

Instructions:

1. Preheat your oven to 400°F (200°C).
2. Wash the potatoes and prick them several times with a fork. Wrap them in foil and place them in the oven. Bake for about 1 hour, or until they are tender.
3. In a mixing bowl, combine olive oil, garlic powder, paprika, salt, and pepper. Coat the tilapia fillets with this mixture.
4. Place the seasoned tilapia fillets on a baking sheet lined with parchment pAper. Bake in the oven for 10-12 minutes, or until the fish flakes easily with a fork.
5. While the fish and potatoes are baking, steam the broccoli florets until they are tender but still crisp.
6. Serve each tilapia fillet with a baked potato (topped with butter, sour cream, and chives) and a side of steamed broccoli.

Fish Taco Recipe Using Leftovers

Prep Time:
20 minutes

Servings:
4-6

Ingredients:

- Leftover tilapia fillets, flaked
- Corn or flour tortillas
- 1 cup shredded cabbage
- 1 ripe avocado, sliced
- 1/2 cup sour cream
- 1 lime, juiced
- 1 tablespoon hot sauce (optional)
- Cilantro, chopped (for garnish)
- Salt and pepper, to taste

Instructions:

1. In a small bowl, mix the sour cream, lime juice, and hot sauce. Add salt and pepper to taste. This will be your taco sauce.
2. Warm the tortillas in a dry skillet over medium heat or in the microwave.
3. Place a portion of the flaked tilapia onto each tortilla.
4. Top the fish with shredded cabbage and avocado slices.
5. Drizzle the sour cream and lime sauce over the top.
6. Garnish with chopped cilantro.
7. Serve immediately and enjoy your delicious fish tacos!

Shrimp Linguini Recipe

Easy Eats

Prep Time:
20 minutes

Servings:
4-6

Ingredients:

- 1 pound linguini
- 1 pound large shrimp, peeled and deveined
- 4 cloves garlic, minced
- 2 tablespoons olive oil
- 1/2 cup white wine
- 1 lemon, juiced and zested
- 1/4 cup fresh parsley, chopped
- Salt and pepper, to taste
- Grated Parmesan cheese, for garnish

Instructions:

1. Cook linguini according to package instructions until al dente. Drain and set aside.
2. In a large skillet, heat olive oil over medium heat. Add minced garlic and sauté for 1 minute.
3. Add shrimp to the skillet and cook until pink and opaque, about 3-4 minutes per side.
4. Pour in white wine and lemon juice. Bring to a simmer and let cook for 2-3 minutes.
5. Toss the cooked linguini in the skillet with the shrimp and sauce. Add lemon zest and chopped parsley. Season with salt and pepper to taste.
6. Serve hot, garnished with grated Parmesan cheese.

Garlic Bread

Ingredients:

- 1 loaf French bread, halved lengthwise
- 1/2 cup unsalted butter, softened
- 3 cloves garlic, minced
- 2 tablespoons fresh parsley, chopped
- Salt, to taste

Instructions:

1. Preheat the oven to 375°F (190°C).
2. In a small bowl, combine softened butter, minced garlic, chopped parsley, and salt.
3. Spread the garlic butter mixture evenly on the cut sides of the bread.
4. Place the bread halves on a baking sheet, cut side up, and bake for 10-12 minutes until golden and crispy.
5. Slice and serve warm with the shrimp linguini.

Simple Salad

Ingredients:

- Mixed greens
- Cherry tomatoes, halved

- Cucumber, sliced
- Red onion, thinly sliced
- Balsamic vinaigrette

Instructions:

1. In a large bowl, combine mixed greens, cherry tomatoes, cucumber, and red onion.
2. Drizzle with balsamic vinaigrette and toss to combine.
3. Serve fresh alongside the shrimp linguini and garlic bread.

Easy Eats

Shrimp Linguini Stir-Fry

Prep Time: 10 minutes | Cook Time: 10 minutes | Total Time: 20 minutes

Servings: 2-4

Ingredients:

- Leftover shrimp linguini (about 2-3 cups) 2 tablespoons vegetable oil
- 1 bell pepper, thinly sliced
- 1 carrot, julienned
- 1 small zucchini, sliced
- 2 cloves garlic, minced
- 1 tablespoon soy sauce
- 1 tablespoon oyster sauce (or hoisin sauce as a substitute)
- 1 teaspoon sesame oil Salt and pepper, to taste
- 1 green onion, chopped (for garnish)
- Sesame seeds (for garnish)

Instructions:

Prep the Veggies:
- Chop the bell pepper, carrot, zucchini, and garlic. Set aside.

Heat the Oil:
- In a large skillet or wok, heat the vegetable oil over medium-high heat.

Sauté the Veggies:
- Add the bell pepper, carrot, and zucchini to the skillet. Stir-fry for about 3-5 minutes until the veggies are tender but still crisp.

Add Garlic and Leftover Linguini:
- Stir in the minced garlic and cook for another minute. Then add the leftover shrimp linguini to the skillet. Toss everything together and heat through.

Season the Stir-Fry:
- Drizzle the soy sauce, oyster sauce, and sesame oil over the stir-fry. Toss well to coat evenly. Season with salt and pepper to taste.

Garnish and Serve:
- Once everything is heated through and well combined, transfer to a serving dish. Garnish with chopped green onions and sesame seeds.

This Shrimp Linguini Stir-Fry offers a tasty and quick way to transform your leftovers into a new and exciting meal, blending the flavors of Italian pasta with the zest of Asian cuisine. Enjoy!

Sautéed Salmon with Rice Pilaf and Steamed Broccoli

Prep Time: 15 minutes
Cooking Time: 30 minutes

Servings: 4

Ingredients for Sautéed Salmon:

- 4 salmon fillets (6 ounces each)
- 2 tablespoons olive oil
- Salt and freshly ground black pepper to taste
- 1 lemon, sliced into rounds
- Fresh dill or parsley for garnish (optional)

Ingredients for Rice Pilaf:

- 1 cup long-grain white rice
- 2 tablespoons unsalted butter
- 1 small onion, finely chopped
- 2 cups chicken or vegetable broth
- Salt to taste

Ingredients for Steamed Broccoli:

- 1 large head broccoli, cut into florets
- Salt and pepper to taste

Instructions for Sautéed Salmon:

1. Season the salmon fillets with salt and pepper.
2. Heat olive oil in a large skillet over medium-high heat.
3. Place the salmon fillets skin-side up and cook for 4 minutes until golden brown.
4. Flip the salmon, add lemon slices around the fillets, and cook for another 3-4 minutes or until desired doneness.
5. Garnish with fresh dill or parsley if using.

Instructions for Rice Pilaf:

1. Rinse the rice under cold water until the water runs clear.
2. Melt butter in a separate saucepan over medium heat and sauté the onion until translucent.
3. Add rice and cook for 2 minutes, stirring frequently.
4. Pour in broth and season with salt.
5. Bring to a boil, then reduce heat to low, cover, and simmer for 18-20 minutes until the liquid is absorbed.

Instructions for Steamed Broccoli:

1. Steam broccoli florets in a steamer basket over boiling water for 4-5 minutes until tender but still bright green.
2. Season with salt and pepper to taste.

Salmon Salad Using Leftovers

Prep Time:
10 minutes

Servings:
2

Ingredients:

- Leftover sautéed salmon (from above), flaked
- 4 cups mixed salad greens
- 1/2 cucumber, sliced
- 1/2 red onion, thinly sliced
- 1 avocado, sliced
- 2 tablespoons capers (optional)
- 1/4 cup olive oil
- 2 tablespoons lemon juice
- 1 teaspoon Dijon mustard
- Salt and pepper to taste

Instructions:

1. In a large bowl, place the mixed salad greens, cucumber slices, red onion, and avocado.
2. Add the flaked leftover salmon to the salad.
3. If using, sprinkle capers over the salad.
4. In a small bowl, whisk together olive oil, lemon juice, Dijon mustard, salt, and pepper to create a dressing.
5. Drizzle the dressing over the salad and toss gently to combine.
6. Serve immediately as a refreshing and satisfying lunch or light dinner.

Enjoy your wholesome and flavorful sautéed salmon dinner and look forward to a vibrant salmon salad the next day, utilizing your delicious leftovers efficiently and tastefully!

Desserts

Dive into the sweet finale of our culinary journey with the "Dessert" chapter, a loving tribute to the timeless joy of baking. Here, we celebrate the simple elegance of a classic vanilla cake, its delicate crumb and the seductive aroma of Madagascar vanilla setting the stage for a variety of sumptuous toppings. Alongside, we pay homage to the rich and moist carrot cake, a tapestry of flavors woven with the warmth of spices, the satisfying crunch of nuts, and the luxurious creaminess of a tangy frosting. Whether you're a novice baker or a seasoned pastry chef, these recipes offer a comforting embrace of tradition and a canvas for innovation. From birthday celebrations to quiet teatime indulgences, this chapter is a testament to the cakes that have graced our tables and sweetened our most cherished moments. So preheat your ovens, and let's turn these time-honored recipes into the crowning glory of your meal.

Vanilla Cake Recipe

Prep Time:
20 minutes

Servings:
4-6

Ingredients:

- 2 1/2 cups (310g) all-purpose flour
- 2 1/2 tsp baking powder
- 1/2 tsp salt
- 1 1/4 cups (285g) unsalted butter, softened
- 2 cups (400g) granulated sugar
- 4 large eggs
- 1 tsp pure vanilla extract
- 1 cup (240ml) whole milk

Instructions:

1. Preheat the Oven: Preheat your oven to 350°F (175°C). Grease and flour two 9-inch round cake pans or line them with parchment paper.
2. Dry Ingredients: In a medium-sized bowl, whisk together the flour, baking powder, and salt. Set aside.
3. Cream Butter and Sugar: In a large mixing bowl, cream together the softened butter and sugar. Beat on medium speed until the mixture is smooth and light in texture (about 5 minutes).
4. Add Eggs and Vanilla: Beat in the eggs, one at a time, making sure each egg is fully incorporated before adding the next. Stir in the vanilla extract.
5. Alternate Dry Ingredients and Milk: Begin by adding one-third of the flour mixture to the butter mixture and beat just until incorporated. Then pour in half of the milk, mixing again. Continue this process, ending with the flour mixture. Ensure everything is well combined but avoid over-mixing.
6. Pour and Bake: Divide the cake batter equally between the two prepared cake pans, smoothing the tops with a spatula. Place in the preheated oven and bake for 25-30 minutes, or until a toothpick inserted into the center of the cakes comes out clean.
7. Cool: Once baked, remove the cakes from the oven and allow them to cool in the pans for about 10 minutes. Afterward, transfer them to a wire rack to cool completely.
8. Decorate: Once completely cooled, you can frost and decorate the cake as desired. A classic choice would be a vanilla buttercream or cream cheese for rosting, but feel free to get creative!

Enjoy your homemade vanilla cake!

Chocolate Cake Recipe

Prep Time:
20 minutes

Servings:
4-6

Ingredients:

- 1 3/4 cups (220g) all-purpose flour
- 2 cups (400g) granulated sugar
- 3/4 cup (75g) unsweetened cocoa powder
- 1 1/2 tsp baking powder
- 1 1/2 tsp baking soda
- 1 tsp salt
- 2 large eggs
- 1 cup (240ml) whole milk
- 1/2 cup (120ml) vegetable oil
- 2 tsp pure vanilla extract
- 1 cup (240ml) boiling water

For the Chocolate Frosting:

- 1/2 cup (115g) unsalted butter, melted
- 2/3 cup (65g) unsweetened cocoa powder
- 3 cups (360g) powdered sugar
- 1/3 cup (80ml) milk
- 1 tsp vanilla extract

Instructions:

1. Preheat the Oven: Set your oven to 350°F (175°C). Grease and flour two 9-inch round cake pans or line them with parchment paper.
2. Combine Dry Ingredients: In a large bowl, sift together the flour, sugar, cocoa, baking powder, baking soda, and salt.
3. Add Eggs and Wet Ingredients: Add eggs, milk, oil, and vanilla extract to the dry ingredients and mix until well combined.
4. Incorporate Boiling Water: Carefully stir in boiling water into the cake batter until it's well combined. The batter will be thin, but this is expected.
5. Bake the Cake: Pour the batter evenly into the prepared cake pans. Bake for 30-35 minutes or until a toothpick or cake tester inserted into the center comes out clean.
6. Cool: Remove the cakes from the oven and allow them to cool in the pans for about 10 minutes. Then, remove from pans and transfer to wire racks to cool completely.
7. Prepare the Frosting: While the cakes are cooling, make the frosting. Combine the melted butter with the cocoa powder in a medium bowl. Alternately add powdered sugar and milk, beating on medium speed to spreading consistency. Add more milk if needed. Stir in vanilla.
8. Assemble the Cake: Once the cakes are completely cooled, spread frosting on top of one cake layer, place the second layer on top, and then frost the top and sides of the cake.

Enjoy your homemade chocolate cake!

Carrot Cake with Cream Cheese Frosting Recipe

Prep Time:
20 minutes

Servings:
4-6

Ingredients:
For the Cake:

- 2 cups all-purpose flour
- 2 tsp baking soda
- 1/2 tsp salt
- 2 tsp ground cinnamon
- 3/4 tsp ground nutmeg
- 1/2 tsp ground ginger
- 2 cups sugar
- 1 1/4 cups canola oil
- 4 large eggs
- 3 cups grated peeled carrots
- 1 cup coarsely chopped walnuts (optional)
- 1/2 cup raisins (optional)

For the Cream Cheese Frosting:

- 8 oz cream cheese, at room temperature
- 1/4 cup unsalted butter, at room temperature
- 1 tsp vanilla extract
- 2 cups powdered sugar, sifted

Instructions:
For the Cake:

1. Preheat your oven to 350°F (175°C). Grease a 9x13-inch baking pan and line the bottom with parchment paper.
2. In a medium bowl, whisk together flour, baking soda, salt, cinnamon, nutmeg, and ginger.
3. In a large bowl, whisk together sugar and oil until well blended. Whisk in eggs one at a time.
4. Add the flour mixture and stir until just combined. Fold in the carrots, walnuts, and raisins.
5. Pour the batter into the prepared baking pan. Spread it out evenly with a spatula.
6. Bake for 40-45 minutes, or until a toothpick inserted into the center comes out clean.
7. Remove from the oven and let cool completely in the pan on a wire rack.

For the Frosting:

1. In a mixing bowl, beat the cream cheese, butter, and vanilla extract together until smooth and creamy.
2. Gradually add powdered sugar and beat until the frosting is light and fluffy.

Assembling the Cake:

1. Once the cake has cooled, spread the cream cheese frosting over the top of the cake in the pan.

2. If desired, sprinkle the top with additional chopped walnuts for texture and decoration.

Slice the carrot cake into squares and serve directly from the pan. Enjoy your sheet pan carrot cake with cream cheese frosting!

Easy Eats

Caramel Cheesecake Recipe

Prep Time:
20 minutes

Servings:
4-6

Ingredients:
For the Crust:

- 1 3/4 cups graham cracker crumbs
- 1/3 cup unsalted butter, melted
- 1/4 cup granulated sugar

For the Cheesecake:

- 4 packages (8 ounces each) cream cheese, softened
- 1 cup granulated sugar
- 1 tsp vanilla extract
- 4 large eggs
- 1/2 cup sour cream

For the Caramel Sauce:

- 1 cup brown sugar, packed
- 1/2 cup heavy cream
- 4 tbsp unsalted butter
- 1/4 tsp sea salt
- 1 tsp vanilla extract

Instructions:
Prepare the Crust:

1. Preheat your oven to 350°F (175°C). Grease a 9-inch springform pan and set aside.
2. Mix graham cracker crumbs, melted butter, and sugar in a bowl until well combined.
3. Press the mixture firmly into the bottom of the prepared pan to form the crust.
4. Bake in the preheated oven for 10 minutes. Remove and set aside to cool. Reduce the oven temperature to 325°F (160°C).

Make the Cheesecake:

1. In a large bowl, beat the cream cheese on medium speed until creamy and smooth.
2. Gradually add the sugar and vanilla, beating until well combined.
3. Add the eggs one at a time, beating just until blended after each addition.
4. Mix in the sour cream until just combined. Do not overmix.
5. Pour the cream cheese mixture over the crust in the springform pan.
6. Bake for 55-60 minutes or until the center is almost set. Turn the oven off, and let the cheesecake cool in the oven

with the door ajar for 1 hour.

Make the Caramel Sauce:

1. While the cheesecake is cooling, combine brown sugar, heavy cream, and butter in a saucepan over medium heat.
2. Stir continuously until the mixture starts to boil. Lower the heat and simmer for about 5 minutes, until it thickens.
3. Remove from heat, add sea salt and vanilla extract. Let it cool to room temperature, then refrigerate to thicken further.

Final Steps:

1. Once the cheesecake has cooled in the oven, remove it and run a knife around the edges to loosen it from the pan.
2. Chill the cheesecake in the refrigerator for at least 4 hours, preferably overnight.
3. Before serving, pour the caramel sauce over the cheesecake.
4. You can add additional toppings like whipped cream, a sprinkle of sea salt, or more graham cracker crumbs if desired.

Slice the caramel cheesecake and serve it chilled. Enjoy the creamy texture with the rich, sweet caramel flavor!

Peanut Butter Caramel Cheesecake

Easy Eats

Prep Time:
20 minutes

Servings:
4-6

Ingredients:

For the Crust:

- 1 1/2 cups of graham cracker crumbs
- 1/4 cup unsalted butter, melted
- 1/4 cup sugar

For the Cheesecake Filling:

- 24 ounces (3 packages) cream cheese, softened
- 1 cup sugar
- 3/4 cup peanut butter (smooth or crunchy based on preference)
- 4 large eggs, room temperature
- 1/2 cup sour cream
- 1 teaspoon vanilla extract For the Caramel:
- 1 cup sugar
- 6 tablespoons unsalted butter, room temperature and cut into pieces
- 1/2 cup heavy cream, warmed
- 1 teaspoon sea salt (optional, for salted caramel)

For the Topping:

- 1/2 cup peanut butter, melted
- 1/4 cup roasted peanuts, chopped (optional)

Instructions:

Crust:

1. Preheat the oven to 325°F (163°C). Grease a 9-inch springform pan and line the bottom with parchment paper.
2. Mix graham cracker crumbs, melted butter, and sugar until well combined. Press the mixture into the bottom of the prepared pan.
3. Bake for 10 minutes, then remove from the oven and set aside to cool.

Cheesecake Filling:

1. In a large mixing bowl, beat the cream cheese and sugar until smooth and creamy.
2. Add peanut butter and mix until well incorporated.
3. Beat in the eggs one at a time, ensuring each is fully incorporated before adding the next.
4. Stir in sour cream and vanilla extract until the mixture is smooth.

5. Pour the filling over the cooled crust and spread evenly.

Bake:

1. Bake for 50-60 minutes, or until the edges are set and the middle still jiggles slightly.
2. Turn off the oven, crack the door open and let the cheesecake cool inside for 1 hour.

Caramel:

1. While the cheesecake is cooling, make the caramel by spreading the sugar in an even layer in a medium saucepan. Heat over medium-high heat, whisking as it begins to melt.
2. Once the sugar has melted, stop whisking and allow the sugar to cook until it reaches a deep amber color, watching carefully.
3. Carefully add the butter pieces and whisk until all the butter has melted.
4. Slowly pour in the warm heavy cream while whisking and boil for 1 minute. Add salt if making salted caramel.
5. Remove from heat and let the caramel cool slightly before pouring over the cheesecake.

Topping:

1. Once the cheesecake has cooled, pour the slightly cooled caramel over the cheesecake and spread into an even layer.
2. Drizzle the melted peanut butter over the caramel and use a toothpick to create a swirl pattern if desired.
3. Sprinkle with chopped peanuts for added texture.
4. Refrigerate the cheesecake for at least 4 hours, preferably overnight, to set completely.

Serving:

1. When ready to serve, remove the cheesecake from the springform pan and transfer it to a serving plate.
2. Slice with a sharp knife, wiping the knife clean between slices to ensure clean cuts.
3. Enjoy your rich and creamy Peanut Butter Caramel Cheesecake!

For a twist, try adding a layer of chocolate ganache on top of the cheesecake before the caramel layer for a luxurious chocolate peanut butter experience!

Pecan Praline Silk Supreme Pie

Easy Eats

Prep Time:
20 minutes

Servings:
4-6

Ingredients:

For the Crust:

- 1 1/2 cups all-purpose flour
- 1/2 cup butter, chilled and diced
- 1/4 cup brown sugar
- 1/4 teaspoon salt

For the Pecan Praline Layer:

- 1 cup pecans, chopped
- 1/2 cup brown sugar
- 1/4 cup heavy cream
- 2 tablespoons butter
- 1 teaspoon vanilla extract

For the Silk Layer:

- 1 cup dark chocolate chips
- 1/3 cup heavy cream
- 1/4 cup powdered sugar
- 1 teaspoon vanilla extract
- 8 ounces cream cheese, softened

For the Topping:

- 1 cup heavy cream
- 2 tablespoons powdered sugar
- 1/2 teaspoon vanilla extract
- Whole pecans for garnish

Instructions:

1. Preheat your oven to 350°F (175°C).
2. Make the Crust:
   - Combine flour, butter, brown sugar, and salt in a food processor until the mixture resembles coarse crumbs.
   - Press into the bottom and up the sides of a 9-inch pie dish.
   - Bake for 15-18 minutes or until lightly golden. Allow to cool completely.
3. Prepare the Pecan Praline Layer:
   - In a saucepan over medium heat, combine chopped pecans, brown sugar, heavy cream, and butter. Stir continuously until the sugar has melted and the mixture is bubbling.
   - Remove from heat, stir in vanilla, and pour over the cooled crust. Allow setting.
4. Make the Silk Layer:
   - Melt chocolate chips with heavy cream in a double boiler or microwave until smooth. Let cool slightly.
   - Whip cream cheese until fluffy. Add

powdered sugar and vanilla, continue to whip until combined.

- Fold the melted chocolate into the cream cheese mixture until no streaks remain.
- Pour this over the pecan praline layer and smooth the top. Refrigerate until set, about 1 hour.

5. Prepare the Topping:
- Whip the heavy cream with powdered sugar and vanilla until tiff peaks form.
- Spread or pipe the whipped cream over the set chocolate silk layer.

6. Garnish:
- Place whole pecans in a decorative pattern on top of the whipped cream.

7. Chill the Pie:
- Refrigerate the pie for at least 4 hours, or overnight, to allow the flavors to meld and the pie to set completely.

8. Serve:
- When ready to serve, slice the pie with a sharp knife dipped in hot water for clean cuts.

Enjoy your homemade Pecan Praline Silk Supreme Pie as a luxurious treat for special occasions or as a grand finale to a family dinner.

Chocolate Chip Cookies Recipe

Easy Eats

Prep Time:
20 minutes

Servings:
4-6

Ingredients:

- 2 1/4 cups (280g) all-purpose flour
- 1/2 teaspoon baking soda
- 1 cup (225g) unsalted butter, room temperature
- 1/2 cup (100g) granulated sugar
- 1 cup packed (220g) light-brown sugar
- 1 teaspoon salt
- 2 teaspoons pure vanilla extract
- 2 large eggs
- 2 cups (about 350g) semisweet and/or milk chocolate chips
- Optional: 1 cup (100g) chopped nuts (walnuts or pecans)

Instructions:

1. Preheat the Oven: Preheat your oven to 350°F (180°C). Line baking sheets with parchment paper or nonstick baking mats.
2. Mix Dry Ingredients: In a small bowl, whisk together the flour and baking soda; set aside.
3. Cream Butter and Sugars: In a large bowl, combine the butter with both sugars; beat on medium speed until light and fluffy. Reduce speed to low and add the salt, vanilla, and eggs. Beat until well mixed, about 1 minute.
4. Add Dry Ingredients: Add the flour mixture and mix until just combined. Stir in the chocolate chips (and nuts, if desired).
5. Prepare the Dough Balls: Drop heaping tablespoon-size balls of dough about 2 inches apart on baking sheets.
6. Bake: Bake until cookies are golden around the edges, but still soft in the center, about 8 to 10 minutes. Remove from oven, and let cool on baking sheet 1 to 2 minutes. Transfer to a wire rack, and let cool completely.

Enjoy your chocolate chip cookies with a glass of milk or simply as a tasty treat!

Simple Sugar Cookies Recipe

Easy Eats

Prep Time:
20 minutes

Servings:
4-6

Ingredients:

- 2 3/4 cups (345g) all-purpose flour
- 1 teaspoon baking soda
- 1/2 teaspoon baking powder
- 1 cup (225g) unsalted butter, softened
- 1 1/2 cups (300g) granulated sugar
- 1 egg
- 1 teaspoon pure vanilla extract
- Optional: 1/2 teaspoon almond extract

Instructions:

1. Preheat Oven: Preheat your oven to 375°F (190°C). Line a cookie sheet with parchment paper.
2. Dry Ingredients: In a small bowl, stir together flour, baking soda, and baking powder. Set aside.
3. Cream Butter and Sugar: In a large bowl, cream together the butter and sugar until smooth and very fluffy.
4. Add Egg and Flavorings: Beat in the egg and vanilla extract (and almond extract, if using) until well blended.
5. Combine with Dry Ingredients: Gradually blend in the dry ingredi- ents. Roll rounded teaspoonfuls of dough into balls, and place onto the lined cookie sheet.
6. Bake: Bake 8 to 10 minutes in the preheated oven, or until golden. Let stand on cookie sheet two minutes before removing to cool on wire racks.
7. Decorating (Optional): Once cookies are cool, they can be decorated with frosting and sprinkles or simply enjoyed as they are.

Enjoy your homemade sugar cookies!

Classic Peanut Butter Cookies Recipe

Easy Eats

Prep Time:
20 minutes

Servings:
4-6

Ingredients:

- 1 cup (250g) creamy peanut butter
- 1/2 cup (113g) unsalted butter, softened
- 1/2 cup (100g) granulated sugar
- 1/2 cup (100g) packed light brown sugar
- 1 large egg
- 1 1/4 cups (156g) all-purpose flour
- 3/4 teaspoon baking soda
- 1/2 teaspoon baking powder
- 1/4 teaspoon salt
- Additional granulated sugar for rolling

Instructions:

1. Preheat Oven: Preheat your oven to 350°F (175°C). Line two baking sheets with parchment paper.
2. Mix Dry Ingredients: In a medium bowl, whisk together the flour, baking soda, baking powder, and salt. Set aside.
3. Cream Butter and Sugars: In a large bowl, beat together the peanut butter, butter, granulated sugar, and brown sugar until light and fluffy.
4. Add Egg: Beat in the egg until well blended.
5. Combine with Dry Ingredients: Gradually stir in the flour mixture until just combined.
6. Shape Cookies: Roll the dough into 1-inch balls and then roll the balls in additional granulated sugar to coat. Place them on the prepared baking sheets about 2 inches apart.
7. Create Patterns: Press each ball with the back of a fork twice to create a criss-cross pattern.
8. Bake: Bake for 10 to 12 minutes or until the edges are light brown. The cookies should still be soft in the centers.
9. Cooling: Remove from the oven and let the cookies cool on the baking sheet for 5 minutes, then transfer to a wire rack to cool completely.

Enjoy your peanut butter cookies with a glass of cold milk!

Easy Eats

Classic Snickerdoodles Recipe

Prep Time:
20 minutes

Servings:
4-6

Ingredients:
For the Cookies:

- 1 cup (224g) unsalted butter, softened
- 1 1/2 cups (300g) granulated sugar
- 2 large eggs
- 2 teaspoons vanilla extract
- 2 3/4 cups (344g) all-purpose flour
- 2 teaspoons cream of tartar
- 1 teaspoon baking soda
- 1/2 teaspoon salt For the Cinnamon Sugar:
- 1/4 cup (50g) granulated sugar
- 1 1/2 tablespoons ground cinnamon

Instructions:

1. Preheat Oven: Preheat your oven to 350°F (175°C). Line two baking sheets with parchment paper.
2. Cream Butter and Sugar: In a large mixing bowl, cream together the butter and 1 1/2 cups sugar until pale and fluffy.
3. Add Eggs and Vanilla: Mix in the eggs and vanilla extract, beating until well combined.
4. Dry Ingredients: Sift together the flour, cream of tartar, baking soda, and salt. Gradually add to the wet ingredients, mixing until a dough forms.
5. Cinnamon Sugar Mixture: In a small bowl, combine 1/4 cup sugar and cinnamon.
6. Shape Cookies: Using a small ice cream scoop or spoon, form balls of dough and roll them in the cinnamon sugar mixture to coat.
7. Bake: Place the dough balls on the prepared baking sheets, spaced about 2 inches apart. Bake for 8 to 10 minutes, until the edges are set but the centers are still soft.
8. Cool: Allow the cookies to cool on the baking sheet for a few minutes before transferring them to a wire rack to cool completely.

These snickerdoodles should come out soft and chewy with a characteristic tang from the cream of tartar and a warm, cinnamon-sugar coating. Enjoy baking and indulging in these delightful cookies!

Strawberry Shortcake

Easy Eats

Prep Time:
20 minutes

Servings:
4-6

Ingredients:

For the Strawberries:

- 1 quart of fresh strawberries, hulled and sliced
- 1/4 cup granulated sugar (or to taste, depending on the sweetness of the berries)

For the Shortcakes:

- 2 cups all-purpose flour
- 1/4 cup granulated sugar, plus extra for sprinkling
- 1 tablespoon baking powder
- 1/2 teaspoon salt
- 1/2 cup unsalted butter, cold and cut into cubes
- 2/3 cup whole milk or heavy cream, plus extra for brushing
- 1 teaspoon vanilla extract For the Whipped Cream:
- 1 cup heavy whipping cream
- 2 tablespoons powdered sugar
- 1/2 teaspoon vanilla extract

Instructions:

Strawberries:

1. In a bowl, combine the sliced strawberries with 1/4 cup of granulated sugar.
2. Stir gently to coat the strawberries in sugar and set aside for about 30 minutes to macerate. This process will help the strawberries release their natural juices.

Shortcakes:

1. Preheat your oven to 425°F (220°C).
2. In a large bowl, whisk together the flour, 1/4 cup granulated sugar, baking powder, and salt.
3. Add the cold, cubed butter to the flour mixture. Using a pastry cutter or your fingers, cut the butter into the flour until the mixture resembles coarse crumbs.
4. Pour in the milk (or heavy cream) and vanilla extract. Stir just until the dough comes together; do not overmix.
5. Turn the dough out onto a lightly floured surface and gently knead it a few times to bring it together.
6. Pat the dough into a 1-inch-thick rectangle. Using a round cutter or a glass, cut out shortcake rounds and place them on a baking sheet lined

with parchment paper.

7. Brush the tops of the shortcakes with a little milk or cream and sprinkle with granulated sugar.

8. Bake for 12-15 minutes, or until the shortcakes are golden brown. Remove from the oven and let them cool slightly on a wire rack.

Whipped Cream:

1. In a mixing bowl, beat the heavy whipping cream, powdered sugar, and vanilla extract until soft peaks form.

Assembly:

1. Split each shortcake in half horizontally.
2. Spoon a generous amount of the macerated strawberries onto the bottom half of each shortcake.
3. Add a dollop of whipped cream over the strawberries.
4. Place the top half of the shortcake on the whipped cream, and add a small dollop of whipped cream and a few more strawberries on top for garnish.

Serve your Strawberry Shortcake immediately for the best combination of textures, from the soft whipped cream to the slightly crisp shortcake. Enjoy the freshness of this timeless dessert!

Apple Cake

Prep Time:
20 minutes

Servings:
4-6

Ingredients:

- 1 1/2 cups (187g) all-purpose flour
- 1/2 cup (100g) granulated sugar
- 1/2 cup (100g) light brown sugar, packed
- 1/2 cup (113g) unsalted butter, softened
- 2 large eggs
- 1/4 cup (60ml) whole milk
- 1 teaspoon baking powder
- 1/2 teaspoon baking soda
- 1/2 teaspoon salt
- 1 teaspoon ground cinnamon
- 1/4 teaspoon ground nutmeg
- 1 teaspoon vanilla extract
- 2 cups (about 2-3 medium) apples, peeled, cored, and chopped

For the Topping (Optional):

- 1/4 cup (50g) granulated sugar
- 1 teaspoon ground cinnamon
- 1 tablespoon unsalted butter, melted

Instructions:

1. Preheat Oven: Preheat your oven to 350°F (175°C). Grease and flour a 9-inch round cake pan.
2. Dry Ingredients: In a medium bowl, whisk together flour, baking powder, baking soda, salt, cinnamon, and nutmeg.
3. Cream Butter and Sugars: In a large bowl, beat together the butter, granulated sugar, and brown sugar until light and fluffy.
4. Add Eggs and Vanilla: Beat in the eggs one at a time, then stir in the vanilla extract.
5. Combine Mixtures: Alternately add the dry ingredients and milk to the butter mixture, starting and ending with the dry ingredients.
6. Fold in Apples: Gently fold in the chopped apples.
7. Prepare Topping: If using the topping, combine the sugar and cinnamon in a small bowl and set aside.
8. Pour Batter: Pour the batter into the prepared pan. If using the topping, sprinkle it over the batter and drizzle with melted butter.
9. Bake: Bake for about 40-45 minutes, or until a toothpick inserted into the center comes out clean.
10. Cool: Allow the cake to cool in the pan for about 10 minutes, then turn out onto a wire rack to cool completely.

Serve your apple cake warm or at room temperature, perhaps with a scoop of vanilla ice cream or a dollop of whipped cream. Enjoy your homemade treat!

Easy Eats

Banana Bread

Prep Time:
20 minutes

Servings:
4-6

Ingredients:

- 2 to 3 ripe bananas, mashed (about 1 1/4 to 1 1/2 cups mashed)
- 1/3 cup (76g) melted butter
- 1 teaspoon baking soda
- Pinch of salt
- 3/4 cup (150g) granulated sugar (1/2 cup if you would like it less sweet, 1 cup if more sweet)
- 1 large egg, beaten
- 1 teaspoon vanilla extract
- 1 1/2 cups (188g) all-purpose flour
- 1/2 cup (122g) unsweetened apple sauce or sour cream (optional)

Instructions:

1. Preheat the Oven and Prepare Pan: Preheat your oven to 350°F (175°C), and with butter or cooking spray, lightly grease a 4x8-inch loaf pan.
2. Mash Bananas: In a mixing bowl, mash the ripe bananas with a fork until completely smooth.
3. Mix Wet Ingredients: Stir the melted butter into the mashed bananas.
4. Mix Dry Ingredients: Mix in the baking soda and salt. Stir in the sugar, beaten egg, and vanilla extract.
5. Add Flour: Mix in the flour.
6. Pour Batter into Pan: Pour the batter into your prepared loaf pan.
7. Bake: Bake for 50 minutes to 1 hour at 350°F (175°C), or until a tester inserted into the center comes out clean.
8. Cool: Remove from oven and cool completely on a wire rack. Remove the banana bread from the pan. Slice and serve.

Optional additions for the batter include chopped nuts (like walnuts or pecans), chocolate chips, or a sprinkle of cinnamon for a spiced variation. Enjoy your homemade banana bread!

Your Input Matters!

Your feedback means the world to me. If you found this cookbook inspiring, practical, or simply mouthwatering, I would be immensely grateful if you could spare a moment to leave a review by scanning the code below. Your honest review not only helps fellow home cooks unlock the potential of leftovers but also provides valuable insights for future editions.

Thank you so much for your support. I wish you a lifetime of success and abundance.

Thank You for Exploring "Easy Eats"

Dear Reader,

As we reach the final page of "Easy Eats," I want to extend my heartfelt gratitude for joining me on this delightful culinary journey. Your presence in the kitchen, whether you're a seasoned chef or a curious novice, has been an integral part of this adventure. I hope that the recipes within these pages have inspired you, brought comfort, and added a dash of joy to your meal times. Your enthusiasm and love for cooking are what make this book truly special. If you've enjoyed your experience with "Easy Eats," I kindly encourage you to share your thoughts by leaving a review on Amazon. Your feedback not only supports me as an author but also helps other food enthusiasts discover the joys of simple, delicious cooking. Visit Amazon to share your review and spread the word about "Easy Eats." Together, let's continue to celebrate the magic of uncomplicated, tasty meals. Thank you once again for your support and happy cooking!

With gratitude,

Brandee Jankoski

Made in United States
North Haven, CT
22 January 2024

47755426R00137